Anatomy of a Park

Anatomy of a

The Essentials of Recreation Area Planning and Design

Albert J. Rutledge, ASLA
Associate Professor of Landscape Architecture
University of Illinois at Urbana-Champaign

Illustrations by Donald J. Molnar, ASLA, NRPA
Landscape Architect

McGraw-Hill Book Company

New York   St. Louis   San Francisco   Düsseldorf   Johannesburg
London   Mexico   Montreal   New Delhi   Panama   Rio de Janeiro
Singapore   Sydney   Toronto   Kuala Lumpur

Sponsoring Editor   William G. Salo
Director of Production   Stephen J. Boldish
Designer   Naomi Auerbach
Editing Supervisors   Gretlyn Blau/ Barbara Church
Editing and Production Staff   Teresa F. Leaden, George E. Oechsner

ANATOMY OF A PARK

07-054347-X

67890 HDBP 754

Foreword

Since about 1900, the play and leisure habits of children and adults in the United States have changed rapidly. Urbanization, with its crowded conditions and constantly developing artificiality, has created environmental modifications which in turn have brought about different leisure-time patterns. Children must learn to play in situations far different than before when there was more formality and closer family supervision. The leisure practices and related social values of adults have also been affected as our technological and economic systems have become more complex.

In recent years, the responsibility for developing play and leisure environments and opportunities has fallen mainly on three groups: (1) landscape architects, planners, and other professionals who design and develop areas and facilities, (2) those who operate, maintain, and develop programs using those facilities—professionals such as recreators, park managers, and recreation and park administrators, as well as technical specialists, and (3) lay persons, members of public boards and commissions. Owners of private recreation enterprises have no less a responsibility and opportunity for this important task of helping to develop programs and facilities that can provide a wholesome and creative leisure-time environment, while at the same time conserving natural resources and beauty for future generations.

Unfortunately, throughout the years, there has been little collaboration between professional designers, professional recreators or park and recreation administrators, and lay persons. These groups have existed in almost independent worlds and have suffered accordingly. Administrators of recreation and park areas and facilities have frequently lacked an effective analysis of their operations. While the recreation profession is beginning to produce, through scientific approaches to management of the leisure environment and better understanding of motivation and human behavior, information which is vital to the designer, the designer has not asked for, or has not recognized the need for, this information. In short, there has been a wide gap between responsible people who cooperatively could bring about a much-needed improvement in our environment for leisure.

This book is intended to bridge that gap. No other publication now exists which approaches this task in such a manner. Written with an appealing organization and style, it unquestionably fills a need now generally recognized. As the author points out, it is meant to stimulate greater collateral action between the designer and his clientele, and to serve as an orientation text for students in recreation and park administration and related disciplines.

A publication as candid and forthright as this may, of course, create some argument. So be it. The lines of communication must be opened. We are challenged to work to better the human condition through cooperative effort and mutual understanding.

Allen V. Sapora, *Head*
Department of Recreation and Park Administration
University of Illinois at Urbana-Champaign

Introduction

*T*his book lays bare the essentials of park design. It is not written primarily for designers, although it may serve them as a refresher or discussion catalyst. Rather, this volume is addressed to nondesigners: lay members of park boards, park directors and superintendents, recreation leaders, faculty and students in university park management programs, the citizenry-at-large. And anyone else whom I may have missed who has this stake in common: You are all the ones directly affected by what a designer proposes for the development of your park lands; you live with the results.

To weigh the potential impact of such results upon you as a park user or agency person, consider simply that all recreation activities need a physical facility. Here is where the bulk of your money is tied up, surfacing first as bond revenue addressed to either land acquisition or construction upon that land. For such large expenditures, should you not expect highest quality? Yet, how often have you accepted dull playgrounds, unsafe swimming pools, or forested areas which have the intrigue trampled out of them the week they are opened? How much of this can be traced to design or lack of it?

Most of your operating budget is put into maintenance. Yet, could not such common problems as erosion, poor drainage, endless trimming of little corners and overgrown areas, and other repairs which take so much maintenance time and personnel have been avoided altogether if they had been dealt with through design before the development was actually constructed?

What can design do to minimize vandalism, discourage lurking undesirables, cut down conflict between autos and pedestrians, and remedy a host of additional problems associated with the public use of land? Many of these questions are answered herein through an introduction to "site design": *a thought process that proposes to anticipate problems of land usage and provide a physical form solution to ensure that the problems never occur.*

There is poor site design as well as good. Needless to say, you would prefer the latter. But can you recognize its essentials? Especially in the paper stage when it costs little to make modifications compared to the complications and expense of making adjustments after the work has been constructed? Can you judge what is the best possible development for whatever circumstances might be at hand?

Sure you can. At least you possess the primary ingredient which will enable you to ensure that your park agency exploits design potential. You have common sense. What is perhaps needed in addition to this is some basic briefing on what constitutes design substance. In this regard, your needs do not extend to the degree that you must become a proficient designer, for as you rely on your attorney to establish your legal bounds and your business manager to strike the best bargain, you may equally expect a professional designer to offer solutions to your facility layout and construction problems.

The knowledge you need is that which will qualify you as a critic of the professional designer's proposal, for you all have the opportunity to play that screening role, spurring park agency staffs toward installing quality works or upgrading subpar developments. If you are an administrator, the designer's plans will come across your desk for signature. If you are an elected member of a lay board or an appointee on an advisory council, plans will be formally presented for your review. Even if you are a citizen without official portfolio—a park user—your voice can be raised in public meetings or through written reactions to pictorial spreads in the news media.

The role of critic is often forfeited by the nondesigner with the rationalization, "The designer is the expert. Who am I to question his efforts?" To repeat: You're the person most affected by the work. You live with the results. If you don't exercise your rights as a critic, you sign a blank check.

The designer should be considered the expert in putting pieces together into a whole. Hire him accordingly. For your own benefit, however, you might readily become the expert in breaking the whole into its contributing parts and evaluating the relative worth of each. And you need not be a master chef to become a discriminating gourmet. In the role of the latter, you may substantially participate in the decision-making process that leads to the development of your park lands.

If at this stage, you see some value in what I am proposing, perhaps you are asking, "Could you supply me with a list of publications on park design and development?" Well, there are many pamphlets and magazine articles dealing with single phases of the subject: technical writings on zoos, golf courses, amphitheaters, stadiums, tennis courts, or picnic areas; symposia proceedings on nature trail layouts, trash can design, or parking lot schemes; construction hints from a superintendent in Minnesota, a designer in Washington, a maintenance foreman in Yellowstone. It would take months of painful research, leafing through hundreds of magazines and soliciting from dozens of agencies, to compile such scatterings. Even if a full listing were available, the question would still remain, "Which one comes first?"

There are several books either totally or partially devoted to the matter, but most of these also focus upon special aspects of development—playground design, marina planning, forest recreation construction, etc. Many of these volumes and the few which attempt to be comprehensive are noted in the bibliography. But despite all that has been done, one element is missing: a basic manual on park design which ties available fragments together and helps make advanced reading meaningful. Without such understanding, where do you begin?

This volume tries to answer that question, for one of its purposes is to provide a framework to which the details of more specific readings can be related. It is proposed as a "nontechnical technical book," hopefully written within the digestive range of the nondesigner, yet with enough substance to be penetrating. Further, this book reflects a designer's mind attempting to supply collaborating professionals with a sense of his objectives and the issues he considers relevant. More specifically, by prying beneath the surface of the grand tour and the fancy rendering to get at what actually makes design succeed or fail, these pages provide information and procedure which will assist in evaluating both completed works and those still in the paper stage.

Emphasis is on evaluating plan drawings, which is the form in which most solutions are presented by designers. The relationship to evaluating constructed works is strong, however; if you can understand what to look for in the drawings, your focus will be sharpened when confronted with a physical work. In turn, acute perception of what causes a completed work to fail or succeed hones your ability to critique the plan drawing.

This might also be a textbook. Augmented by tales from experience, slides, plans, and field trips, this book could serve as an outline guide to presenting an understanding of park design to majors in the fields of park management and recreation programming. This could also provide organizational material for the preparation of short-course seminars for professional administrators and other agency personnel.

This book, then, is meant as a foundation. For a basic briefing on park design and development, this is where you might begin.

Albert J. Rutledge

Contents

Foreword   v
Introduction   vii
Acknowledgments   xii

1. Context: Past and Present   1

2. The Umbrella Considerations   13

3. The Aesthetic Considerations   35

4. The Functional Considerations   53

5. Plan Interpretation   81

6. Site Design Process   91

7. Plan Evaluation   107

Etcetera   143
Appendix 1   Selected Park and Activity Size
                    and Facility Standards   146
Appendix 2   Recreation Demand Questionnaire   148
Appendix 3   Leisure Behavior, Attitude,
                    and Opinion Questionnaire   149
Appendix 4   Selected Game Area Size Standards   163
Appendix 5   Selected Game Area Layout Diagrams   164
Appendix 6   Responses of Selected Trees to Recreation Use   165
Appendix 7   Responses of Selected Soil Types to Recreation Use   166

Bibliography   173
Index   177

Acknowledgments

*S*pecial notes of gratitude are due to Helen Peterson, who as an elected park commissioner was the first to ask me the question, "Could you supply me with a list of publications on park design and development?" out of which was born the concept for this book.

To my wife, Cathy, who helped in the sorting out of ideas and, with unflagging patience, listened critically to the reading of draft chapters.

To Don Molnar, who not only livened this volume with his artistry, but contributed significantly to the creation of the case studies as well.

To landscape architects Bill Carnes and Gene DeTurk and recreator Al Sapora for their suggestions and commentary, with additional thanks to Gene for permission to feature his school-park master plan and Al for his contribution of the Foreword.

To Walt Keith, President of the Urbana Park Board, Lowell Fisher, President of the Urbana School Board, Joe Bannon, Chief of the University of Illinois Office of Recreation and Park Resources, Ken Schellie of Schellie Associates, Inc., and Rhodell Owens, Director of Parks and Recreation, Peoria Park District, for permitting the use of documents prepared through their offices.

To Kathy Henson and Donna Schultz for their cooperation in typing and editing what must have seemed to them to be an endless number of drafts.

chapter one

Context : Past and Present

$\mathcal{W}$e are in an age of specialists. This is good, for it allows subject matter to be probed and applied in depth. But specialization has its drawbacks as well, since many disciplines have so developed in depth that their implications frequently cannot be understood by people in adjacent fields. As a result, experts are often isolated from the potential contribution of others.

In today's complex society, no single discipline can pretend to solve substantial problems without collaborative assistance from those in allied fields. Accordingly, this book proposes to foster an understanding of design and designers among park administrators, recreation leaders, and others responsible for park development. All of us must perform as a team if quality works are to become widespread.

While it may seem reasonable that a team relationship should exist, it is missing in too many cases. To some extent, lack of collaboration is due to the professional isolationism brought about by the speciality phenomenon. Much of it can also be traced to what can be described as a historic hangover. Therefore, history warrants review and evaluation as to its contemporary relevance.

FROM OLMSTED TO TODAY

It should be no surprise that park and recreation policy makers and landscape architects are often allied when one realizes that we have the same parent: Frederick Law Olmsted (1822–1903). It was Olmsted who, in describing his role as designer-superintendent of New York City's Central Park, conceived the title "landscape architect" and applied it for the first time in the mid-nineteenth century to those who organized land and objects upon it for human use and enjoyment. It was also Olmsted, with the development of Central Park, who initiated the first concentrated park and recreation movement in the United States. (See Fig. 1.1.)

Out of these beginnings emerged three related phenomena: a design style for America suited to nature-oriented parks; a split of recreation authorities into two camps of opposition, passive recreation enthusiasts and active recreation advocates; and a situation whereby landscape architectural schools provided many park authority leaders.

In part, these traditions were rooted in a revolution which occurred in England preceding the development of Central Park. Nineteenth-century industrialized England was laced with dirty, sinful, poverty-stricken, run-down cities. As a psychological counterthrust, England moved into its Romantic period, its people escaping from their oppressive environment through songs and poems of fantasy.

The well-to-do, utilizing their financial advantage, escaped physically, fleeing with their families and belongings to the countryside. There they called upon designers to plan their country estates. Sensing a desire for relief from every reminder of the city, designers strove to create patterns which excluded the axes, circles, squares, and other manifestations of geometry with which the city was visibly organized. They discovered the alternative in nature and began to lay out roads, walks, and other use areas in the "loose" organizational systems associated with

1·1 *Frederick Law Olmsted (R), the nation's first landscape architect, designed Central Park (L) and supervised the early stages of its construction.*

nature, rather than with the regimented forms deduced from the mathematically oriented minds of their predecessors. Sweeping lawns and meadows appeared. Man's works were fitted to existing land configurations. Plants were allowed to exhibit their natural forms. As shown in Fig. 1.2, the acreage took on a relatively undisturbed "natural" appearance despite the inclusion of man-made necessities.

Olmsted found himself in a situation somewhat parallel to that in England. In the 1850s, New York City was also industrialized

1·2   The English Romantic style of landscape design.

and highly choked. While Olmsted was sensitive to the "English solution," he was equally concerned with the plight of the common man. Reasoning that the entire population could not flee to the countryside, he proposed that, within the heart of the city, there should be rural landscape where a man could go quickly to "put the city behind him and out of his sight and go where he will be under the undisturbed influence of pleasing natural scenery."[1] Working with this principle in mind, he collaborated with English architect Calvert Vaux in a competition to design Central Park. The Olmsted-Vaux plan won, and Olmsted stayed on to oversee the construction.

Olmsted was an extraordinary man, Central Park (the first planned park in this country) being but the beginning of his contributions to open-space planning and development in the United States. Subsequently Yosemite Valley in California was set aside as the first state park. Its preservation was brought about as a result of a report Olmsted compiled in 1865 on the natural wealth of the region. Shortly thereafter, Olmsted conceived the idea that municipalities should link a series of parks into a working complex, thereby evolving the concept of a park system. His influence in this regard is still evident in such cities as New York, Buffalo, Philadelphia, Boston, and Washington, D.C., the lands proposed by him for incorporation into these systems being the backbone of what is available today. He was also the creator of the parkway concept, having advanced the idea of this type of roadway to connect Riverside (which he designed as the country's first residential subdivision) with Chicago in 1869.

Olmsted's superior ability to blend roads, buildings, walks, etc., into the existing landscape without visible disturbance led to emulation by other outdoor area designers, now called landscape architects. While they provided a legacy we enjoy today, many became trapped by the style that proved so successful for Central Park. While such naturalized developments were well suited to passive and semiactive types of recreation, they were decidedly more difficult to justify for active sport facilities, especially when these were located in little corners of the urban scene where segments of unassuming nature might appear

[1] Charles E. Doell and Gerald B. Fitzgerald, *Brief History of Parks and Recreation in the United States,* The Athletic Institute, Chicago, 1954, p. 33.

strangely out of place, even if possible to install at all. It was also argued that active sports and related activities had little need for being surrounded by rustic trappings. Accordingly, the landscape architects of that time and many into the twentieth century either shunned the design of active sport facilities or attempted to stuff them into a rural mold.

On the recreation side of the ledger, Olmsted was a persuasive champion of his cause that the essential recreation need was for rural retreats in the heart of the city. This became *the* park and recreation movement of the times. As the movement grew in acceptance, another came along. Physical education enthusiasts proclaimed that recreational pleasures could also come from planned exercise, skill development, and the excitement of competition. Rather than cooperate, Olmstedian naturalists and active recreationists became wrapped up in the virtues of their own causes and formed poles not only of thought but of administrative authority as well.

"Parks" became defined as naturalized passive retreats. "Park departments" became solely concerned with parks as defined above. Landscape architects (schooled in the Olmstedian tradition) turned their energies to park development and, in their enthusiasm for the topic, included options in park management in their university programs. Such background led landscape architects not only to the design of park areas in the early part of this century, but to roles as park administrators and policy makers as well.

Concurrently, "recreation areas" became defined as active-sport-oriented facilities—playgrounds, hard-surface court areas, team sport fields, etc. Municipal "recreation departments" were formed separate from park departments to handle only recreation areas and on the policy level were staffed by those with a physical education background. As a result, "parks" received much design attention, "recreation areas" very little. Unfortunately, one can only conclude that such separation and loss of interdisciplinary collaboration resulted from nothing more significant than professional pique.

This hangover remained relatively intact until after World War II when it became jostled by new demands. Population upsurge and unparalleled economic expansion focused eyes upon the question of land usage in its broadest sense. Accordingly, landscape architectural education expanded its horizon in order to cope with the contemporary complexities of any type of land-use problem: subdivision, campus, industrial complex, active *and* passive park, plans for whole cities and regions. To make room for new design inputs, many schools dropped park management as an option for their landscape architectural students.

At the same time, population pressures and increases in leisure time raised serious questions about the depth and scope of the recreational experience. The same population upsurge hastened purchases of public park land to the point that heretofore sleepy park agencies awoke abruptly as complex managerial concerns. In reaction, university programs in park administration and recreation research were expanded and many more formalized as recognized entities with highly sophisticated missions.

Today, we are left with the vestiges of the historic hangover; some park departments are still not speaking to recreation departments. But there is a growing movement toward combining both responsibilities under one administrative roof. This new philosophy, which minimizes duplication of efforts and recognizes that leisure-time needs can be satisfied through both active and passive means, is implied by Charles Doell in a few simple definitions. Doell, Superintendent of Parks Emeritus of the Minneapolis park system, sets forth "recreation" as "refreshment of the mind or body or both through some means which is in itself pleasureful"[2] and defines "park" as a "piece of land or water set aside for the recreation of the people."[3]

Agencies are also witnessing an influx of university-trained administrators who are inheriting the roles formerly filled by landscape architects, engineers, horticulturists, and others who once moved from their related interests to management posts. The intensive background in management which the new administrators possess has been gained at the expense of technical prowess in some areas, thereby increasing their reliance upon on-the-job advice from others in such fields as design, construction, maintenance, etc. While much technical problem solving must now come through the collaborative route, what remains as before in the hands of the administrators by virtue of their

[2] Charles E. Doell, *Elements of Park and Recreation Administration*, Burgess Publishing Company, Minneapolis, 1963, p. 3.

[3] *Ibid*, p. 5.

continuing positions at the top of the table of organization is final approval of and the ultimate responsibility for the acts of their consultants and staff.

Meanwhile, in recognition of the contemporary philosophy, landscape architects have equalized their attention to facilities for both passive and active recreation pursuits. In the past few decades, mainstream designers have gained the habit of designing land-use units on their own merits, having purged from their thinking style preconceptions which previously led many to stuff design elements into nonconforming molds.

FACING THE PRESENT

In contemporary thinking, appropriate design is that which meets objectives considered particularly relevant for the individual park site under study. This is not to say that broad goals common to many park situations do not exist. Such matters as good land drainage and efficient circulation must be satisfied in all solutions. What this thinking does imply is that design criteria should be ordered through analysis of each situation rather than through reflection upon what has been found to be applicable to other circumstances. From this it follows that, even where some objectives repeat themselves often enough to be considered common to all developments, the manners in which they are best satisfied are most likely to be unique. Each park has differences in site character at least. Hence, since what may be appropriate in one situation may not suffice for another, suspect the design solution which appears to be a rubber stamp etched from a prior scheme.

The unique requirements of a particular circumstance can only be discussed with information related to that job in front of us. Before dealing with such specifics, however, it will be useful to set forth those objectives which have been found to be common to most developments. To do so, let us first identify some basic environmental needs which, if met, could benefit all of us in the middle of the twentieth century. This look around us is in keeping with what history has taught. Recalling that the movement from geometric to nature-oriented design arose out of a desire to disassociate with the city, it may be concluded that meaningful work is done in response to the times.

Superintendent Doell has proposed that the recreational experience is one of pleasure. This suggests that we should search out some pleasures which have been erased from the contemporary scene which can and perhaps should be made once more available through physical development.

Visual refreshment comes immediately to mind. A quick glance at our present surroundings reveals what distressed Olmsted 100 years ago: clutter, ugliness, and uninspiring drabness broken here and there by screaming chaos (Fig. 1.3). The present-day building boom with its back-to-back developments has caused this visual pollution to proliferate way beyond the scope of Olmsted's day. What he knew as an urban problem now infects whole countrysides. Blank reaches of asphalt. Blaring signs. Ugly shapes and unpalatable forms. Choked roadways tangled around walking routes. Junk. All like dirty dishes in the sink (Fig. 1.4).

Since we are always in environment of some kind, we cannot help but react to it. Behaviorists maintain that surroundings consciously or subconsciously shape our attitudes, breeding tranquility or tension, pleasure or dissatisfaction. It is, therefore, reasonable to surmise that too much of our present environment adds tension to tension, firing the already hectic stresses of job, home, and everyday modern existence.

Olmsted's parks were for escape. But is this entirely possible today? The shoddiness which our unlimited mobility takes us past daily is overwhelming (Fig. 1.5). How lasting is the momentary relief of a park experience if one must return to face that which in such great proportions drove one to escape in the first place? Parks can no longer be thought of primarily as vehicles for escape. Rather, they should be developed to serve as exemplars of what is possible in terms of soul-satisfying environment and catalysts for promoting higher works in other types of developments, toward the day when everything which man builds contributes to positive physical surroundings. Design of recreation areas, therefore, must address itself to more than simply the supply of a facility. At worst, it should not serve up an additional pollutant, in reality breeding tension while in theory proposing to relieve it. At best, it should strive for the provision of visual refreshment not only for those who engage in the activity within, but for those who pass by daily as well.

Mental exercise appears to be another need of our times. Our mass-production systems which have provided us with a wealth

1·3　*Blight in the city.*

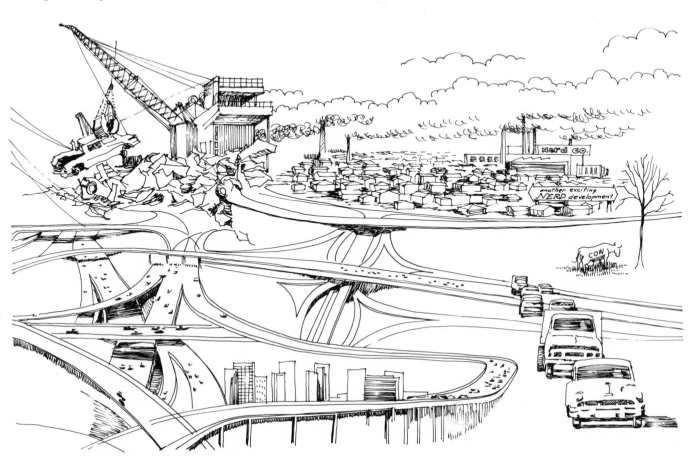

1·4　*Chaos in the countryside.*

of goods have at the same time created an environment of sameness in how we live, what we use, etc. Uninterrupted monotony can dull the brain. It can lead to mental lethargy. This does not happen when the mind is continuously called upon to act. When it is subjected to differences, comparisons are made, capacities to distinguish are exercised, curiosity is developed. To counter the contemporary phenomenon of creeping boredom, design should strive to provide environmental diversity by ensuring that each development turns up unique.

Sameness also leads to a loss of identity, for most of today's products are made to reflect the characteristics of the "average" person and are carved out of responses such as that of the man with his head in the oven and his feet in the refrigerator who concludes, "On the average, I feel comfortable." The average person does not exist. Thus, products framed in his image are addressed to no one in particular.

Pride, pushing aside the hollow feeling of anonymity, can result from being surrounded with things of close association. Hence, design should attempt to give a development a "personality" with which its users can identify—something truly "mine" as differentiated from "yours."

Up to a point, people can get used to anything, be it air pollution or environmental drabness. But the adaptability of the human makeup, while on the one hand allowing us to adjust to adverse conditions, on the other hand can threaten our survival, for it makes us so accustomed to damaging circumstances that we don't really notice them—until, perhaps, it is too late to reverse their steamrolling inertia. In his book, *So Human an Animal,* biologist René Dubos maintains that many diseases have originated from deleterious environmental influences to which man has *seemed* to become adjusted. What long-run havoc will reign over us if we continue to take our chances with surroundings that breed tension, monotony, and anonymity?

While some may still wish to argue about the consequences of denying the pleasures cited, there is an additional contemporary issue which will be decidedly more difficult to debate. We are witnessing a competition for land unparalleled in history: land for the subdivision, factory, school, shopping center, golf course, bridle trail, and an infinite number of other needs. In the search for acreage, vested interests are militantly striving to outfox others in order to gather in their required land area. Others be

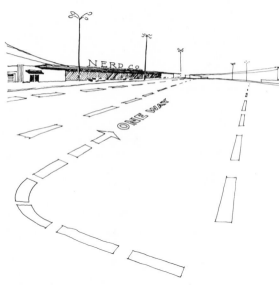

1·5 Bleak and barren and devoid of compassion for the human condition.

damned. Too often, this blind competition leads to improper use. Facilities are ending up on sites more suited for other purposes. And these purposes are finding themselves left with no land appropriate to the satisfaction of their needs. In the rush, sight has been lost of the fact that land is limited and that its unbuilt-upon reaches are diminishing rapidly.

This is not just happening to "other people"; it is everybody's local problem. In the Midwestern corn and soybean belt, tree cover is a premium. The town of Urbana, Illinois, once stood as an exception, for it was blessed with 6,400 acres of prime forest —its "Big Grove." Today, only 300 acres remain and much of this is scheduled to go under to make way for industrial development. So, muscled out of land well suited to their needs, park agencies are left with naught but flat and barren fields.

Wise land-use judgments are critically needed, for—as dramatized in Fig. 1.6—1 million acres, approximately the equivalent of the state of Rhode Island, are being bulldozed each year. There must be assurances that each interest will be satisfied, but only on land appropriate for its use. Errors in assigning use to land

1·6 *"The good Lord is makin' more people, but he ain't makin' no more land."* . . . *Will Rogers*

is a luxury of the past. Mistakes cannot be abandoned. No longer is there a similar site down the road.

CONTEMPORARY DESIGN GOALS

Every action begins with the identification of objectives or what is to be accomplished. While no two design projects are ever alike, each having differences of site, facilities, users, etc., there are always present in every project several goals which remain constant.

In the most general sense, foremost is the provision of facilities which lend grace to the environment, provide mental stimulation, have pride-inducing personality, and make best use of land. These are traditional needs, but they are singled out for special focus here because of the sad superabundance of facilities which do not satisfy these requirements and the urgency to do something about them before the population—numbed into resignation to the inevitability of that which is truly unnecessary—become lemmings well on their way to the sea.

Within this contemporary context, there can be identified further common objectives to be met in the design of park properties. In the following chapters, these are offered as "principles" or broad guideline categories in which judgments must be made as the designer proceeds through the problem-solving process. The principles are equally applicable to sites for passive uses as well as for active functions. They are addressed to the satisfaction of general contemporary needs as well as to the specifics of individual projects.

Under each principle are listed "matters of concern." These are a breakdown of the principles into parts and are additional points to weigh when considering the variables of each project.

Principles and matters of concern are the "whats." Illustrations are laced throughout to indicate a few "hows," manners in which principles might be satisfied and ways in which the matters of concern might be treated. Since it is impossible to set down every possible circumstance, illustrations are meant to merely indicate the wide range of opportunities for principle satisfaction. In addition, the appropriateness of the "hows" must be considered on the merits of the cases in which they are presented. Quite reasonably, what satisfies for one instance might not work for another.

chapter two
The Umbrella Considerations

*T*his first set of considerations stands for a broad overview of what guides design decisions. It comprises the overarching principles to which all other goals must relate.

PRINCIPLE 1: EVERYTHING MUST HAVE A PURPOSE

If wise land use is essential, there is no room in site design for whimsical judgments, even though many moves may come to the designer through his intuition. Intuition is only a means, a mental short-cut, to solution, but it is not a justification for results. Decisions held out for acceptance can and should have convincing back-up. They must be supported by sound and logical reasons.

Design, therefore, must have purpose. One such purpose is to establish appropriate relationships between the various parts of the park complex. These parts include: *natural elements* (land, water, plants, etc.); *use areas* (game courts, ball diamonds, parking lots, roads, walks, maintenance yards, etc.); *major structures* (buildings, dams, etc.); *minor structures* (drainage, electrical and other utilities, fences, benches, drinking fountains, signs, etc.); *people;* and other *animals*. In addition, all are affected by *forces of nature* (wind, sunlight, precipitation, etc.) (See Fig. 2.1.)

While each part will present its singular demands, no part can work in isolation from another. Follow steps A–F, Fig. 2.2 and note that, for instance, sun orientation affects the location of the amphitheater, for the sun must not shine directly in the eyes of the audience (A). The amphitheater siting directs the placement of the parking lot (B), which narrows down the possibilities for access routes to the public streets (C). The amphitheater parking lot could serve the nearby marina, but the marina noise, in turn, must be neutralized before it reaches the amphitheater (D). The traffic invited to this amphitheater-marina complex must not raise havoc with surrounding land uses as would occur if it proved a safety hazard for children crossing neighborhood

2·1 *A park is a complex of many parts.*

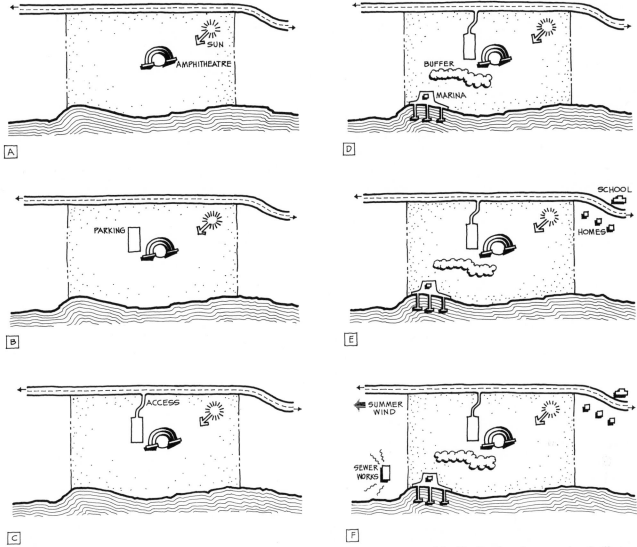

The location of every park unit affects the workability of another.

streets (E). In the reverse, the smells, noise, and visuals emanating from surrounding facilities must not cause the enjoyment of theater going or boating to be lessened (F).

Interdependence among all the parts must be recognized and accommodated if any single part is to work. Consideration of such relationships extends from the broadest determination of the park's place in the city plan to the smallest decision about where to place the trash basket.

2·3   Use areas may require different degrees of slope.

Matters of Concern

1A. Relation of Park to Surroundings   Design focus must go beyond the limits of the park's boundaries in order to answer such questions as: Will the proposed park development cause flooding in the valley below? Will it cause traffic to back up into residential streets? Will the arrangement of the new facilities replace the pleasant view of undeveloped land with an unpalatable distraction? Will the location of play areas encourage baseballs to fly into backyards?

The reverse, the impact of the surroundings on the park, is equally significant. Will adjacent land uses send stomach-churning odors across proposed picnic areas, create safety hazards, or encroach upon park serenity? In a positive sense, do the surroundings offer potentials to be "borrowed"—a good view, a major access route, a utility source?

By purposeful design measures, a sharp designer exploits the advantages of surroundings and overcomes the limitations posed by adjacent lands and their uses. He attempts also to see that the park remains the best of neighbors, never causing the usability of surroundings to be diminished.

1B. Relation of Use Areas to Site   Land cannot be wasted. Every corner of every site must be assigned a use. This does not necessarily mean active use. Lying fallow, land may serve as a buffer or a viewing panorama. It may be left as conservation acreage if it has been determined that active trespass would cause loss of wildlife cover or vegetation that holds back flood waters. Even an undisturbed swamp serves a valuable purpose, for its porous surface allows rainwater to penetrate and refill underground reservoirs. Fill in or pave over the swamp, and the water supply for neighboring habitations diminishes.

Whether they be for active or passive uses, *facilities should be assigned only to portions of the site that are compatible with that use.* As an example, consider the implications of a single site factor, degree or steepness of slope. As demonstrated in Fig. 2.3, tennis courts cannot function unless they are on flat land. Tobogganing must be matched to relatively steep pitches. While neither tennis nor tobogganing do well on precipitous slopes, these grades are ideal for separating two nonconforming activities such as a temperance meeting and a brewery company picnic.

All uses can be cataloged as to their demands for slope and much more: type of soil (stability, fertility, permeability), need for vegetative cover, nearness to water, utilities, and transportation, orientation to sun and wind, to name a few.

Therefore, it is essential in design to identify both the limitations of the site and its potentials, to overcome the former in the location of facilities and exploit the latter. To bring this point home, see Fig. 2.4 and consider the consequences if use areas are not located where site characteristics are compatible: picnicking is designated for the sun-baked field, while nearby trees are cleared for the parking lot; buildings are constructed on shifting soil bases, while intermittent walking routes are laid out on adjacent stable surfaces; the amphitheater is situated in a howling wind tunnel, the winter roads where the snow loads are heaviest, and the ballfields in the marsh.

1C. Relation of Use Areas to Use Areas Before being assigned to locations on the site, various uses should be analyzed in terms of compatibility with each other. Such an analysis unearths both common and disparate threads among the units. For instance, as illustrated in Fig. 2.5, nature walks, canoe lagoons, and spooning nooks can be considered alike for they are quiet and soul-satisfying, whereas tennis courts, handball surfaces, and basketball pavements are related because they are noisy and sweat producing. Because the latter possess these characteristics, they are in opposition to the quiet grouping.

By locating common units together and segregating them from noncompatible use areas, activity enjoyment is enhanced; such distractive battles as noise versus quiet are eliminated. In addition, movement orientation is simplified. Those with an interest in one type of activity need proceed to only one area to find a full range of sought-after pursuits. Area supervision is also assisted. A single supervisor can keep track of, say, preschoolers if all of their activity areas are grouped together, whereas more

2·4　*The results when use areas are located on unsuitable portions of the site.*

personnel would be required if such play zones were scattered all over the site. And maintenance procedures are simplified. Since like activities usually require similar maintenance chores, performance time can be minimized if trash trucks, horticultural equipment, infield draggers, honey wagons, etc., are able to concentrate upon close-together areas.

In weighing similarities among use areas, sometimes clearcut decisions can be made. Most often, however, use areas are found to be interdependent for one reason, but incompatible for another. For instance, maintenance yards conflict visually with picnic sites, but movement between each must be of short span; parking lot noise detracts from the concert, but the lot must be located nearby; playground complexes are for kids, but for supervisory purposes must be associated with adult areas. However conflicting, all such demands must be treated in the use area organization proposal. Perhaps in the latter example, the playground could be physically separated from the adult station by a low barrier yet, over the barrier, remain visually evident for supervision.

After use-area-to-use-area relationships are decided upon, the design task becomes one of finding site situations which fit the desired pattern; for example, for picnicking a well-drained sector with ample shade trees and stable soil lying next to a cleared patch suitable for parking but away from the school building situated just outside the park's limits. (See Fig. 2.6.) Thereby an "ideal" relationship is struck in accordance with all three matters of concern discussed so far: use areas to use areas, use areas to site, park to surroundings.

1D. Relation of Major Structures to Use Areas In a sense, a building may be thought of as a use area and decisions regarding its location made in accordance with considerations already stated. Special attention should be paid to the relationship of various rooms to adjacent outdoor areas. This will raise such questions as: Is the gym entrance immediately handy to the playfield? Can the children move from the kindergarten to the totlot without having to cross the parking area? Are classrooms buffered from noisy game facilities? Can nonswimmers move from the bathhouse to the wading area without having to walk along the edge of the deep pool?

1E. Relation of Minor Structures to Minor Structures Just as a park is a complex of related areas, each use area is a complex of in-

2·5 Compatible uses should be located together yet be separated from groups of disparate activities.

terdependent physical elements. As secondary as these concerns might be when weighted against the other relationship matters, inattention creates rightful public irritation. Is the bench close to the refreshment stand? Or must Mom juggle a half-dozen ice-cream cones for 100 yards before she is able to sit down among her brood? Is the seat near enough to the light fixture which is supposed to illuminate its surface? Is it the right distance from the trash basket, thereby accommodating the easy flip of the discarded newspaper? If the basket is in an inconvenient location, the paper is going to stay on the bench waiting for the wind to blow it all over the site.

The Key Word

Establishing ideal relationships is only one purpose of design. Other purposes will be articulated later. For now, consider that this introduction to relationships has been set forth to illustrate the broader point that every design move must be made for a logical reason. To ferret out other purposes and to guard against arbitrary judgments and half-baked conclusions, the simple question to ask of a designer is, "Why? What is your purpose?"

From the broadest concern ("Does this facility belong in this part of town?") to the most incidental detail ("What underlies the selection of that material, color, shape, height, width?"), expect "why" to be answered to your fullest satisfaction.

PRINCIPLE 2: DESIGN MUST BE FOR PEOPLE

People are the benefactors of any park development. Right? Then why is development success so often measured entirely by how well it meets the demands of machines and equipment,

2·6 An "ideal" use relationship.

2·7 *Roadway design should meet both the demands of the auto and the needs of the people inside.*

how it simplifies administrative paperwork, and how it fits an unyielding formula of quantitative standards? Perhaps it is because some minds have become immune to the fact that these impersonal matters are merely means to serve people, not ends in themselves.

The elevation of impersonal matters to prime measures of development success can lead to the creation of an uncomfortable mold into which people must be forced. This conflicts with design purpose, which in this case is to develop an environment which fits people.

Matter of Concern

2A. Balance of Impersonal and Personal Needs
While it is essential to meet the requirements of machinery, that is not enough. For instance, in the design of roads and parking lots, it must be recognized that the automobile demands a certain road alignment, gradient, roadbed structure, and curb height, as well as a 10- by 20-foot paved slab for storage. It must be remembered at the same time, however, that the *person inside the auto* seeks visual refreshment and mental exercise. As exemplified in Fig. 2.7, these could be provided for him by roads rhythmically curving between softly rounded earth shoulders, focusing upon appetizing views, with peripheral distractions screened and oppressive natural elements shaded out—as he wheels over proper alignment, up and down appropriate gradient, between suitable curb heights, and into the parking lot.

Accordingly, the demands of the auto, the gang mower, the utility network, etc., must not overshadow the needs of the people whom these inanimate objects propose to serve. Both sets of requirements must be given substantial due.

Administrative efficiency is another essential in the park agency operation, and it is often met through the purchase of standardized equipment. Certainly, it is simpler to fill out an order blank for 100 standardized items than to requisition a like amount of individual units, and it is economically beneficial to purchase mass-produced equipment. But what happens when the result is that everything looks alike, looks alike, looks alike? Mental stimulation is suppressed. Identity is smothered in anonymity.

An example of standardization run amuck is the "typical" playground. Always the same swings, the same teeter-totters, the same slides. Sameness dulls visual appetites, including those of adults who are there to supervise the kids or who pass alongside every day. Of direct effect upon the children is the fact that such stock items can be used in only one fashion. Such rigidity of use defeats their purpose, for the child's discovery mechanisms are stifled.

When can the economic benefits of standardization and mass production be realized without cheating the prime benefactor or the person? Consider dovetailing the previous principle into this one by applying the key word, "why?" What is its purpose? If playground apparatus is to stimulate a child's imagination, equipment that offers only dulling regulated usage is unacceptable. Yet, a park bench, upon which one is expected only to sit, might reasonably be mass-produced if it proves comfortable, and look-alike items might be distributed about the park if the visual effect of their sameness is submerged in unique overall development. This is another reason why rubber-stamp layouts should be avoided so that the standardized parts of the scheme will be only incidental portions of a refreshingly individual whole.

In addition, for a purpose such as the giving of information, standardization can actually benefit people. Since repetition creates familiarity, similar styles among signs and waste receptacles, for example, provide immediate signals for someone in the time of need. Because one has seen and identified the object with a particular function before, in searching he knows what he is looking for. His familiarity helps him to spy it quickly (Fig. 2.8).

An impulsive urge to standardize has also led to the preparation of tables which propose types of facilities and activities for

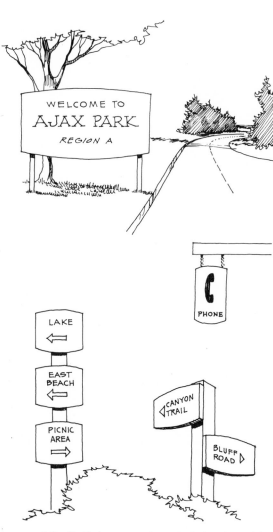

2·8 *Similarity among sign styles helps the traveler in search of a message.*

typical park properties. Since these "quantity standards," based upon national averages, are found in almost every book dealing with the design of recreation areas, there is no need to issue a complete tabulation here. (See the sampling included in Appendix 1.) However, it is relevant to this discussion to forewarn about the blanket application of those standards which tend to impersonalize development. For no matter how flexibly they may be labeled, there is always present the temptation to regard them as absolute; as a substitute for thinking, they appear to offer an easy path to solution.

For example, consider the suspicion raised when one leading standard developer suggests that preschool areas should have chair swings, a sandbox, a small slide, and a simple climbing device, and then, in the next breath, proposes identical forms of equipment for older children's play areas—only larger. Can it be that children from tots to teens have the same play needs? Or do tots, teens, unmarrieds, parents, senior citizens, etc., have disparate demands?

Another standard proposes that each neighborhood park contain a softball diamond, playground equipment, multiple-use pavement, and a turf area. But do not parks for the economically deprived require elements for types of activities different from those for parks serving the more secure middle class? Are conclusions related to Chicago equally valid in East Podunk?

Obviously, any development responsive to people has activities and facilities tailored to the clientele at hand. This is more likely to come from recreators with a finger on the pulse of the locale and on-the-spot research than from impersonal generalists drawing lists in their rocking chairs far removed from the scene.

To gather a more personalized list of activities and facilities, the responsible recreator conducts local "demand studies" through questionnaires and interviews. (See examples in Appendixes 2 and 3.) Since responses to questionnaires most likely point only to known alternatives, trial-and-error systems are also attempted whereby activities are initiated to test local interest in matters with which the residents might be unfamiliar.

While such procedures tend to bring development closer to people, a nagging weakness remains; demand studies do not express every facet of need. Whatever a person says he wants springs from a need and should therefore receive substantial attention from those in a position to provide for it. However, rare is the person who possesses enough insight to identify every condition which could bring benefit to him. Accordingly, it is incumbent upon professionals working in the fields of human activity to take up where public articulation falters, folding into their work livability factors seldom expressed in public proclamations. Realistically, the science of sorting out veiled phases of human need is inexact at best, and its application is often held back by the ever-present fear of becoming a self-righteous moralizer rather than a servicing prophet by mistaking a purely subjective conclusion for one which indeed does contribute to the common good. However, recent questions raised by physiologists, psychologists, sociologists, anthropologists, ethologists, and others attempting to understand human behavior point to areas within which leisure-time experts can be operating, translating reasonable hypotheses and theories into activity programs.

The recreator might be pondering: Is the rhythmic exercise of jogging and bicycling more beneficial than the forceful yet erratic energies spent in such physically explosive games as tennis? Do our present social problems suggest that in their play, children should be taught to cooperate rather than to compete? How can recreation affect the family structure? Do not many commonly accepted sports overly stress sword discipline, whereas they ought to be encouraging responsibility? Is the concept that leisure time provides relief from workaday drudgery an anachronism in light of the preponderence of laborsaving devices that now distinguish our culture? Should not the move be toward developing creativity which laborsaving devices tend to smother?

As a sign of growing maturity in the recreation field, some universities are turning their research activities to the identification of needs. Toward the possibility of consequential breakthroughs, it behooves more educators to research needs, more researchers to write, and more practicing recreators to heed the consequences of the work. For, after all, if literal demands were the only criteria for activity programs and facilities, parks would be big television sets and the prime activity pot parties.

The vagaries of human needs haunt the designer as directly as they do the recreation administrator, for there is equal motivation in design work to respond to more than literal public clamor. While the recreator is asking what mental and physical benefits are to be gained from activity involvement, the landscape architect seeks to understand the sociological, psychological, and physiological effects of surroundings and incorporate such findings into his work. This is because he knows that unless he can relate his work to the satisfaction of human needs, he cannot really state that he is "developing an environment which fits people," which is what landscape architecture is all about.

Knowledge about the effects of the environment upon human behavior is still in the speculative stage among the scientists to whom the landscape architect looks for data which can be translated into physical development. Although the pace of movement in the twilight of speculation is far from ideal, it is beginning to stir a dialogue. Among designers, questions are being raised about the implications of such concepts as "territoriality." Popularized by ethologist Robert Ardrey, author of *The Territorial Imperative,* this concept suggests that each human instinctively drives to gain an area of space as his exclusive possession, guarding it with unusual ardor against intrusions by other members of his kind. Could the neighborhood park be within the territorial purview of nearby residents? Is there a gut reaction against agency ideas for its use and development as being intrusive? To resolve the territorial imperative, should the people be closely involved in the planning of facilities and activities beyond the roles of critics and questionnaire respondents? How can professional expertise and lay voice be blended to bring this about?

The concept of territoriality is not accepted by many of Ardrey's peers, especially those on the opposite side of the age-old nature- (that we act out of instinct) versus nurture- (that environmental factors mold our actions) debate among behaviorists. However, the critical questions such a concept raises among designers are driving them to seek further evidence which ultimately should bring pressure upon the behaviorists to seek further themselves, their infighting potentially tempered by the large body of thought which reasons that human behavioral patterns spring from an interwoven play of *both* instinctive and environmental factors.

Such searching points up that, although human need in its pure state is the province of sociologists, psychologists, et al., they cannot isolate themselves from the applied professionals such as the landscape architect and the recreator if anything is to be accomplished on the basis of scientifically deduced find-

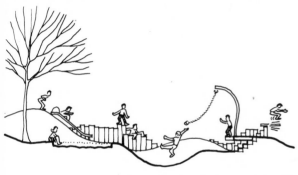

2·9 *Organizing play pieces so as to provide experience continuity fulfills an observable play pattern among children.*

2·10 *Where playground devices are isolated from one another, the potential for continuous play experiences is diminished.*

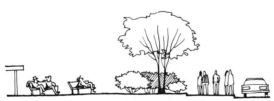

2·11 *Derelicts may wish to be isolated from the eyes of passers-by.*

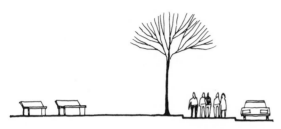

2·12 *The empty benches might mean that park users wish privacy.*

ings. The ideal effort is a collaborative interplay among researchers and appliers, which is another reason why there are so few specifics to date. Such highly knit collaboration is sorely lacking, held back in some cases by the same kind of professional pique which once separated park and recreation people.

Even where there is an appreciation of mutual contribution, too often one side hibernates waiting for the other to act first. It is quite popular among landscape architects to hang all the blame on the behaviorists because "They do not put information in form which designers can understand." While there is much truth to this, it does not hide the fact that constructed design projects are ideal laboratories in which landscape architects themselves may gather empirical evidence on behavior. More designers should simply observe their own works in use. And if they see that children have placed planks between play devices and are enthusiastically crawling, jumping, swinging, and wrapping themselves around them, continuously moving from one device to another innovating along the way, they might conclude that for optimum play fulfillment all playground pieces should be connected rather than separately spotted about, as is presently the most common practice. (See Figs. 2.9 and 2.10.)

If they see that derelicts disappear once a park has been cleared to permit viewing from the street, they might speculate that the most comfortable environment for the derelict is one that is screened from the world of the affluent. As a result, they might design sitting areas for "Bowery" clientele as well-buffered islands, rather than as zoo cages open on all sides to the eyes of curious passersby. (See Figs. 2.11 and 2.12.)

As in any empirical endeavor, success involves not only perception before the fact, but also many subsequent inspections of the constructed works to observe whether the speculation has indeed proved out. So there really isn't any reason for designers to hibernate. Conclusions gained from observing the people actually using developments can right now be woven into the thinking toward improving future works of a similar type.

There are also several elementary theories extended by behavioral scientists which lend themselves to immediate translation into physical development. These, too, may readily be confirmed through observation. For instance, many behaviorists contend that we all have a psychological need to shy away from circumstances of potential pain or injury. As a result, designers should go to great lengths to separate vehicular from pedestrian traffic patterns as is the case shown in Fig. 2.13. This is in addition to the fact that it is decidedly more pleasant to walk in an environment devoid of belching automobiles.

Also suggested is the need for companionship or being with others. To designers of outdoor areas, this could imply that convenient gathering places should be a part of every development. This is especially significant for park properties, which, as public nodes, are ideal vehicles for both visual and verbal interaction from the obvious—sharing experiences with friends —to the more obscure—silently measuring the cut of another's jib. One might argue, therefore, that a park does not have to be jammed full of equipment, game courts, and directed things to do to satisfy a basic human need. Viewing and being with people may be as significant as engaging in formal games.

This might also cast some fresh light on the cry that too many people are spectators and not enough are activists. Perhaps people should be decidedly both, with loitering itself given as much due as structured recreation. To the designer, this could suggest that convenient spaces for social gathering should be set aside in every park regardless of its prime function and that every facility should be designed to encourage human interaction. This could extend from the simple provision of a bench to sculpturing the land to orient it for sitting purposes to "where the action is," as is illustrated in Fig. 2.14.

Where interaction is to be encouraged, benches should be grouped to face each other (Fig. 2.15), never back-to-back or isolated singly. In addition, distances between benches are important to conversation making, as has been indicated to us by Robert T. Hall in his book *The Silent Language.* Anthropologist Hall points out that members of different cultures automatically assume unique distances when conversing, and he lists what he has found to be the most comfortable talking distances between Americans. In his book *Personal Space: The Behavioral Basis of Design,* psychologist Robert Sommer reports that back-to-back and far apart placement of seats is a technique used in airline terminals to drive people from the waiting areas into bars and coffee lounges where the atmosphere is more conducive to conversation. (Not too coincidently, this is where the terminal can make a buck as well.) Therefore, if you see park benches arranged like those in transportation terminals—and most of

2·13 *Automobiles and pedestrians should be separated.*

2·14 *Orientation of sitting places toward activity spots encourages human interaction.*

2·15 *Grouping of benches fosters conversation making and silent inspection of others.*

them are—you may conclude that the designer wants to discourage interaction or drive visitors into bars or didn't know what he was doing when he ordered the benches set out (Fig. 2.16).

Freedom, to be unencumbered by domineering authority and chart one's own course, has been identified by some behaviorists as another human need. As will be discussed in the chapter dealing with circulation, landscape architects can meet this requirement by organizing facilities and traffic ways so as to guide visitors into use patterns with which they can agree, rather than force them to move about only as others demand. Freedom also suggests a need to provide space which is unallocated to predetermined activities. As exemplified in Fig. 2.17, these would be arenas for satisfying whim, "do as you damn well please areas": throw a ball, pick a flower, chase a greased pig, or do whatever suits your fancy at the moment. This will be discussed further when we speak of use freedom and control.

Mental exercise and pride, previously identified as worthy of

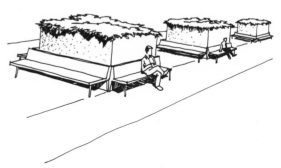

2·16 *Isolation of benches hinders being with others.*

2·17 *Simple open space should be set aside to satisfy the leisure-time whim of the moment.*

design attention because of opposing environmental trends, have also been mentioned by human-need scientists. To provide for the exercise of the senses and to satisfy a need to ask, answer, formulate, and analyze, designers can enrich projects with fascinating details and provide surprises—an unanticipated opening to a view, a bubbling pool or other discovered feature set in a hidden place, etc. To engender pride or satisfy the need to be recognized and command the respect of others, landscape architects can ensure distinct design for each project and strive toward well-maintained and efficiently functioning units. They can also personalize areas with characteristics familiar to the user, thereby establishing a development with which he can readily identify. Thus, nondecorative design would be provided for puritans versus flamboyant design for extroverts. We will have more to say about personalizing areas in Chapter 3, "The Aesthetic Considerations."

Tricky in its own right, this task of satisfying behavioral need in design is further complicated by the fact that each of the foregoing requirements appears to have an equally strong contradictory partner. Need to avoid circumstances of possible harm must be paired with challenge or need to show evidence that one can take care of himself. Companionship is coupled with solitude or desire to have some time alone. Freedom has its counterpart in security or lack of anxiety.

While these needs are held out to be common to all of us, it is reasonable to assume that certain ones would require more intensive consideration than others in particular land-use circumstances. Clearly, behavioral scientists should be a part of every project team to prepare social profiles of the people whom the park will serve from which these insights might be drawn. Their trained eyes are also needed in the observation of use both before and after development is completed. Thorough research into the habits of animals to ensure an environment tailored to their needs preceeds the design of every modern zoo. People deserve as much. Yet, collaborative consideration of human habits as they might be accommodated in design for people is not presently common practice.

However, designers need not wait for collaboration to become honed. Cursory, yet—as a first step—significant commonsense evaluations are not too difficult to evolve. Several matters appear worthy of serious consideration in most if not all projects; mental exercise and the securing of identity certainly rank high among them. In addition, our present social problems suggest that places for interaction should be incorporated into every work. The difficulties of predicting the full range of needs for the variety of clientele found in a public park lead to the thought that areas for free expression are always a must. There are also needs which are related to very practical circumstances—avoidance of harm where life and limb are in unquestionable danger or security where circulation tangles guarantee loss of direction are undoubtedly priority matters in all such cases.

Analyses of user or use then can lead to specific determinations as to which of the needs should receive the most design attention for a particular job. From a social profile could come information that the facility will serve gregarious folk, and hence companionship would follow as a primary design criterion. In contrast, solitude might be the essential design requirement for introspective souls. As has been stated, such profiles should happily come one day from behaviorists so that all the nuances might be caught. But even now, designers who live with the people or otherwise know the people or *make up their minds to do so* can develop much of the necessary feeling for the human situation. At least, designers should not ignore clues thrown down in front of them. In a recent conversation, a landscape architect marveled at the panoply of bright colors exhibited in the dress and other physical symbols of an ethnic gathering. Yet, the brightest color found in a major renewal development which he designed for their neighborhood was a tepid grey. The designer admitted two things: The people identified with bright colors; they hated the new development.

Where a social profile is impossible to pin down, attention might be directed to the use on the assumption that users will come to the facility in a frame of mind associated with the activity, and it is their expectation that should be fulfilled. Hence, challenge might be conceived to be essential for the playground, and freedom rated highest where the unspoiled dimensions of nature are to be experienced.

The criteria unearthed through these analyses become objectives to be met in the physical design of the place and to be considered by decision makers when weighing alternatives otherwise equal. For instance, solitude as the goal might direct the designer to minimize vehicular penetration of the site, whereas without this criterion in mind he might have been free to intertwine roadways all over the park. Often the contradictory partner reads as strong as the prime consideration and must be given equal acknowledgment. Thus, while a designer might introduce intimate enclosures to satisfy a dominant desire for solitude, he might at the same time ensure that they are readily accessible to congregating spaces in order to meet a momentary urge for companionship.

The realm of human need requires much more empirical data and theory capable of testing in the laboratory of actual use before its potential can be fully harnessed as design criteria. Let's wish those working in this area much success. For it is suggested that, if people could be psychologically soothed by their physical environment, they might be released from many of the tensions which plague them constantly and thereby be able to perform more effectively in their daily tasks. This possibility alone should be enough to command designers, recreators, and others who deal with resources for people to seek out the behaviorists and the behaviorists to move toward closer collaboration with their applying counterparts.

The Key Word

Attention to people is another "why" or purpose underlying many design moves. Toward determining the reasonableness of a site design scheme, it can therefore be said: Where the limitations and requirements of mechanical devices are determinants, where economic and administrative efficiency is a consideration, where average standards are held out as the magic answer, indeed, where any action is ostensibly taken to provide for people, the key word is simply "people." Is the satisfaction of their needs *the* priority criterion in the development?

PRINCIPLE 3: BOTH FUNCTION AND AESTHETICS MUST BE SATISFIED

If we surround ourselves with specialists because we believe they probe deeply into subject matter, we should expect more from their efforts than quantity. Specialists' products must also have that inherent mark of excellence called *quality*.

Site design quality requires two returns. The first is highest dollar value, that which can be measured in terms of hard cash. Evaluation of highest dollar value is simple. Weigh the relative costs of alternative solutions. If the problem is surface drainage and blacktop will generate the necessary flow, it is monetarily foolish to consider brick with its greater expense.

But highest human values—that which is judged in terms of human response—must also be measured. These values, adding or detracting from a person's well-being, are found in the intangible influences possessed by every tangible object. They might stem from a tantalizing view, the roll of swelling topography, the shade of a tree, or the intrigue of a paving pattern. While the value of human response to such matters cannot be price-tagged, it can very well be determined inwardly.

Matter of Concern

3A. Balance of Dollar and Human Values To bring quality into park design, both dollar and human value aspects must be weighed. These aspects boil down to *functional* considerations (upon which the dollar sign can be placed) and those of *aesthetics* or beauty (from which pleasureful human response is gained). Therefore, our blacktop-versus-brick dilemma cannot be resolved solely by the application of a cost factor.

Toward striking a balance among dollar and human values, matters of function and those of aesthetics are solved concurrently in design. Hand-in-hand. Never apart. (See Fig. 2.18.) Facets of aesthetics are never thought of as window dressing applied after function has been solved; functional matters are never treated as evils forced in after some pretty picture has been established. The sense of such togetherness in the design process will be illustrated in subsequent chapters as it will be shown that many moves which can be termed aesthetic actually strengthen the functional side of the solution. Accordingly, as design strives to balance dollar and human values, so too should evaluation. The relative success of a scheme should be measured in both contexts.

The Key Words

Every design solution must possess workability. That is, every tangible object and relationship system proposed must function in the most efficient manner possible. Therefore, judgments regarding highest dollar value or top degree of function can be wrapped around the term "efficiency." In evaluation, this becomes the word which provides a test for every one of the site's

2·18 The land drains well and steps accommodate the grade change (function), while the paving patterns satisfy visual appetites (aesthetics).

working parts. At the same time, the word "experience," in its cerebral context, can be used to trigger critical thoughts about the aesthetic success of the same parts.

Matters of aesthetics address themselves to the refreshment of the mind as set forth in this definition of beauty: "An emotional response in the mind of the beholder that to him is pleasureful." When this definition is overlaid upon Mr. Doell's idea of recreation, "refreshment of the mind or body or both through some means which is in itself pleasureful," the tie between aesthetics and park development becomes not only obvious, but bound fast.

Aesthetic quality becomes known to you through your senses; that is, you must see, smell, hear, touch, and/or taste something before it can have influence upon you. Accordingly, that which is charged with aesthetic duty must capture the attention of your senses. It must not rely upon contrived intellectualizing for its essence to emerge; it must generate an impact that makes its presence unmistakably felt. On the other hand, if its perceptual message is so weak it remains unnoticed, you will come away from it without gain, the result being akin to the experience of sucking on a straw in an empty glass. Nothing.

Triggered by the word "experience," measuring the aesthetic success of any development begins with the asking of the following questions in turn: Is there a sensory experience provided? Is it strong and influential? Is is pleasureful?

TO MORE SPECIFIC CONSIDERATIONS

Attention to purpose, people's needs, function, and aesthetics are the umbrella considerations which spread themselves over the entire period of design thinking. The key words: "why," "people," "efficiency," and "experience" focus attention upon basic issues with which the designer contends and, therefore, comprise the tests which must be passed by every development commitment.

Nestled under the umbrella are more detailed principles which also guide design decision. In the ensuing chapters, these additions will be presented under the labels of "aesthetics" and "function," for it is in the course of solving problems of experience and efficiency that actual project purposes, people's needs, and dollar and human requirements are identified.

Aesthetics and function are separated herein for discussion purposes only. It must be remembered that in the design process they are woven together in deference to their interdependence.

chapter three
The Aesthetic Considerations

*T*o weave aesthetic quality into a development, a designer applies not only principles of art composition but his powers of intuition as well. The possession of the latter is a must. For in such a complex field as aesthetics, there exist so many factors capable of modifying each other that it is impossible to set down, much less follow, rules that never vary. Yet, it is not necessary to possess this mysterious capacity in order to discriminate between the pleasing and the displeasing. The unschooled observer can readily gauge the aesthetic reasonableness of any development if he simply sharpens his powers of awareness.

The initial step in honing awareness is to establish extremes on a mental "excellence scale" as you go about the environment. Although beauty may be hard to describe, you certainly know when you are within its influence; for instance, you would probably not find it too difficult to rate the relative aesthetic merits of Frankenstein's monster and a candidate for the *Playboy* centerfold. It should, therefore, be this easy for you to come to conclusions about a blank-paved, junk-filled playground in contrast to one with stimulating layout and imaginative equipment.

To know the best, you should also experience the worst. Thus, never at any stage of shopping for excellence should you feel you have seen all. To remain alert, always be on the lookout for that which is a notch below what you have previously considered poorest. But also continue to expect that which is above the best you have heretofore seen. Developments you are directly concerned with can then be appraised against the extremes on the scale in this mental catalog.

To establish degrees of excellence (or offensiveness) among those developments which lie between the extremes, provisions for *order* and *variety* should be measured. While "beauty is in the eye of the beholder," order and variety are psychological appetites which most behaviorists agree are common to all beholders. Regardless of its other attributes, an aesthetic composition must possess these if there is to be present a possibility for generating a pleasureful response.

The need to perceive order or a logical correctness about what is experienced stems from man's need to understand and find reason and regulation in his works. Under an orderly influence, the mind experiences tranquility. All is right with the world. Everything fits into place. One can go about his meaningful activities without being disturbed by the surroundings.

The desire to witness variety or contrast, a touch—but only a touch—of disorder, difference, or change from the expected is rooted in man's need to exercise his senses. Variety provides excitement and stimulation. It is the spice that combats boredom. It also keeps the faculties alert, thereby honing them for other tasks of daily decision making.

Yet, overabundance of either in the environment is equally distressing. If regulation is too obvious or too much of the same thing is apparent as in Fig. 3.1, the scheme becomes tiresome. Monotony ensues. Conversely, if contrasts ricochet about in unending fashion as in Fig. 3.2, the result is unnerving chaos which feeds mental distress.

In a successful design, both order and variety are present in fragile equilibrium. Note in Fig. 3.3 that there is just enough

3·1 *Overabundance of uniformity results in monotony.*

3·2 *Excessive dissimilarity breeds chaos.*

3·3 *Order and variety in balance.*

order to suggest logic and stability, coupled with the right amount of dissimilarity among the parts to vitalize the situation. Primarily, it is the designer's intuition that directs him to the appropriate mix; one may state, "Designing is like preparing a fine stew by ear."

To measure provisions for order, the following criteria can be applied. Whether or not the proper amount of variety has been instilled, however, must be left to the critic's personal judgment. To help tune up your ability to make that judgment, comments regarding variety will be interjected wherever opportunities arise.

3·4 *Invigorating: an expression inherent in nature.*

PRINCIPLE 4: ESTABLISH A SUBSTANTIAL EXPERIENCE

The first step toward understanding or sensing reason—perceiving order—in a work is the placing of a label upon it. It is answering the question: "What is it?" This is why you see titles on abstract paintings. They are the artist's concession to the general public.

Since it is impractical to hang labels upon a physical development, the development itself must have such strong character that it renders an impression capable of being identified. As illustrated in Fig. 3.4 such impressions are distinctly etched in nature. Because of characteristics expressive of what they are, we have come to label natural units as prairie, desert, lake plain, "Marlboro Country," etc., and are immediately able to distinguish one from another.

The same thing is possible among man's works as is pointed out in Fig. 3.5. Each man-made unit is capable of evoking an emotional image whose influence could cause one immediately to label it "peaceful" or "exciting" or "awesome" or whatever else might appear to fit. If the radiating image is strong enough to be so labeled upon first contact, it will quickly capture the mind's attention, thereby maximizing the possibility that the development will provide the experience which the label implies. What can cause such substantial expressions in constructed works?

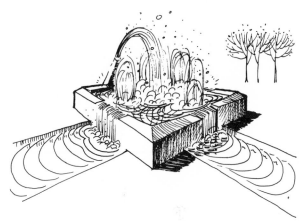

3·5 *Exhilerating: an expression within the capabilities of man to produce.*

Matters of Concern

4A. Effects of Lines, Forms, Textures, and Colors   The raw materials of site design are not trees, land, and paving materials, but things whose presence is as real as those material objects (see

3·6   The raw materials of design.

3·7   Straight lines.

Fig. 3.6): *lines* (single edges indicating directional movement), *forms* (external appearances of objects defined by lines making closed circuits), *textures* (distribution of lights and darks over surfaces caused by inconsistencies in illumination), and *colors* (qualities of light reflected off surfaces as defracted by the eye's prism). These are the raw materials of any artist, as was inadvertently admitted by James McNeill Whistler when he insisted that we call the famous painting of his mother "Arrangement in Gray and Black." Whether found in Whistler's work or on the trees, land, and paving materials with which a landscape architect deals, lines, forms, textures, and colors possess the potential for producing emotional effects.

Consider first the potential inherent in lines and forms. (Since a series of forms, rhythmically leading the eye to and fro attain the directional tendencies of line, both can be investigated interchangeably as to the production of effect.) Straight lines are bold and domineering; they move the eye forcefully (Fig. 3.7). On the other hand, horizontal forms are peaceful, calm, and at rest, for they lie comfortably on the ground at harmony with gravity (Fig. 3.8). Ninety-degree vertical lines possess a dynamic quality as they move the eye upward; the more attenuated the form, the more forceful the movement, and hence the greater the uplifting sensation of soaring (Fig. 3.9). Diagonal and zigzagging lines are active and spirited, for there is lots of erratic movement in many directions (Fig. 3.10). Curved and undulating lines are not as dynamic as zigzags. Being slow and meandering, they are inclined to be gentle and tranquil (Fig. 3.11). But if the curve changes direction rapidly, it can produce an animated or gracefully spirited feeling (Fig. 3.12).

Pronounced rough textures are bold and domineering like straight lines and, in the extreme, ponderous and primitive (Fig. 3.13). By contrast, fine textures are inclined to be sprightly and a bit fussy. Since fines are more subtle than rough textures, they can produce a more casual effect (Fig. 3.14).

Bright and high value colors are gay, lively, and spirited (Fig. 3.15). Deep hues are somber and mellow (Fig. 3.16). Neutrals (greys and browns) recede to the background and are therefore useful in separating clashing colors, toning down the potentially hectic effect of many unrelated hues. This is why stage designers often use neutral backdrops against which to play the bright costumes of many dancers. When applied to buildings and

3·8   *Horizontal forms.*

3·9   *Vertical lines.*

3·10   *Zigzagging lines.*

3·11   *Gently curving lines.*

other dominant facades, this premise might be equally successful in separating out the conflicting hues of city neon.

Color any development cautiously. Since color appeals to the most primary instincts—consider the attraction of both children and savages to red cloth and bright beads—its sensational qualities are the first influences felt. Thus, where the reading of lines, forms, and textures is essential to the scheme, color must be used with some restraint, for if strewn about with heavy-handed abandon, it will overpower everything else at the scene.

Every material object, whether it be fence, shrub, trash can, piece of playground equipment, or body of water, exhibits line, form, texture, and color. That is, through these elements, all ordinary things have aesthetic potential. It remains for the landscape architect to harness that potential in order to produce an emotional effect.

4B. Effects of Dominance   To exploit their potential, the designer acts from an understanding that the aesthetic elements are never experienced alone, but in relation to one another. It is seldom that the pink bloom of a tree is disturbingly garish by its mere presence, but it may be if it clashes with nearby blues and yellows. Accordingly, the designer must contend with the qualities of all objects from every viewpoint as one might move about.

One reason why you gain only marginal impressions from many man-made developments is that, as you move through them, you do not contact enough objects which exhibit like qualities. For instance, in an outdoor restaurant, there may be present a scattering of signboards with bright cheerful colors, but their impact is watered down by the existence of an equal proportion of dumpy furnishings and somber-appearing material in the same vicinity. Having equal visual importance, each divergent quality neutralizes the other, and there ensues little emotional reaction to either.

But what happens when, through creative action, most objects within visual range are made to exhibit similar characteristics? Say, bright cheerful colors on the signboards and sun umbrellas, fine textures in the plantings, sprightly dappled areas of light and dark provided by grillwork, and comically pulsating water in the fountains. They all contribute and add up to the provision of an exhilarating atmosphere. Whereas contrasting qualities might be interspersed for variety's sake, they should occur in restrained amounts to remain subservient to the one emotional feeling which has been allowed to *dominate*. As demonstrated in Fig. 3.17, the development now has a coherent expression. It says essentially one thing. It can be labeled. And most important, because the lines, forms, textures, and colors are, each in its own way, making a similar statement, the development's expression stands a good chance of being felt.

However, because visual focus is never static—the eye continually swings about bringing new objects into view—additional moves to intensify the dominant effect are necessary in order to ensure that it does indeed capture the mind. There must be measures taken to see that the eye focuses on only material objects which have the dominant qualities and does not stray to things which radiate other expressions.

3·12 *Spiritedly curving lines.*

4C. Effects of Enclosure The simplest move is to wall out the irrelevancies. Consider, for example, the room in which you are reading this material. The walls screen out hallway distractions. You are, therefore, forced to address yourself only to what the room contains, receiving an impression that it is dreary, exciting, peaceful, or whatever.

Enclosure by walls, ceilings, and floors aids in putting the dominant effect across. It does much more. Beyond serving to assist the performance of lines, forms, textures, and colors, *enclosure itself* brings psychological influence to bear upon the confined person.

3·13 **Rough textures.**

The effects of enclosure are hardly ever consciously appraised, but it remains that you are affected by being enclosed even though you may be absorbed in other pursuits. A parallel example can be drawn by an allusion to music. It is not necessary to listen consciously to a tune in order to be caught up in it. Many supermarket people know this well. Throughout the day, they pipe in dreamy melodies to encourage a slow shopping pace, thereby generating shelf browsing. But near closing time, they step up the tempo with such tunes as "Stars and Stripes Forever," because the help wants you out so they can go home.

Two basic aspects of enclosure play upon the subconscious of the confined. The first is *volume* or the amount of "emptiness" which surrounds you. Picture the feeling that evolves from and between extremes. Feel yourself encased in plaster. Proceed to being shut up in a closet. Then move to the den of a "typical" home. The degree of comfort generated at these various stages is

3·14 *Fine textures.*

directly related to the amount of surrounding volume. Arrive at an amount minimally comfortable for a single person, and you have a room suited to introspection: the den.

For contrast, associate yourself with maximum volume: an empty room twice the size of the Houston Astrodome. Consider sitting therein, and it should be immediately apparent that this is not a volume suited to individual meditation. You may receive an initial sensation of awe. But this will soon degenerate into discomfort as there arrives the sudden realization of your smallness in relation to the vast amount of volume which surrounds you.

The second influencing aspect is *type* or form of the enclosure. While there are many variations, most enclosing forms can be placed in three basic categories. There is first of all static or complete enclosure. As it is usually of a square or circular nature, a static volume does not move. It is inactive. It just sits there. As such, it is well suited to functions which require isolation or attention to the center—a discussion on enclosure, for example.

On the other hand, linear enclosure is an elongated volume that moves in a definite direction and is open at both ends. Since the volume moves in a direction, so will the eye of the person contained within it, making it logical for him to proceed physically on the insinuated tack as well. Therefore, while a linear volume is not conducive to inward-oriented activities, for the motion of its volume might be distracting, it is well suited to movement or circulation: a hallway. At the end of its tunnellike form, you might find a static enclosure: a room. The completeness and lack of movement of the terminating volume signifies a definite end to the journey.

3·15   *Bright colors.*

3·16   *Dark colors.*

3·17   *A strong aesthetic statement is made when all objects within visual range are made to exhibit complementary qualities.*

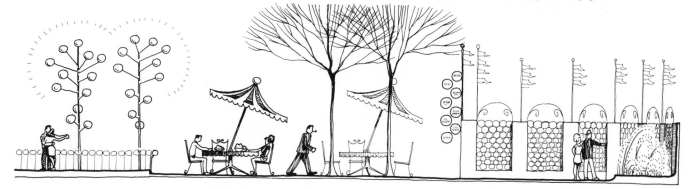

3·18 *The outdoor environment is three-dimensional.*

3·19 *The planes which enclose outdoor spaces.*

3·20 *Static space.*

The third type, free enclosure, is a meandering volume which allows movement of the eye in any number of directions. It is suited to unregimented activities where individual choice is being encouraged. Free enclosure is seldom found in buildings, although occasionally you may have come across free-flowing "roomless" houses which allow even the children to roam about at will, giving them the impression that all is theirs, too. A house laced with these uninhibited volumes is also a great place to throw parties.

However, the point is not to dwell upon architecture, but to use building rooms and hallways as introductory examples of what is faced by landscape architects in the outdoors. Such a devious route to the issue appears necessary, for while everyone understands that interior rooms are enclosed, few recognize that the outdoor environment is as three-dimensional as the indoors. (See Fig. 3.18.) A prime purpose of outdoor area design is not simply to devise two-dimensional ground patterns, but to create three-dimensional volumes so that the aesthetic and functional advantages of enclosure might be gained.

In the jargon of the landscape architect, exterior rooms are called "spaces." The floors of these exterior spaces are termed "base planes" and can be comprised of earth, water, low-growing vegetation, and all varieties of paving materials. Walls are called "vertical planes" and can be laid up with stone, concrete, fencing, trees, shrubs, and building facades. The ceilings are designated "overhead planes" for which can be used overhanging tree branches, pergolas, man-made cantilevers, and even the sky.

In addition to containing their occupants and providing the various sensations of enclosure, the spatial planes serve necessary functions. As illustrated in Fig. 3.19, the base plane takes traffic. Where vertical planes are above 5 feet in height (eye level), they can be sight, noise, wind, and sun barriers. Below this height, vertical planes still form physical deterrents and thus can help to guide circulation. Overhead planes provide additional shelter from the natural elements.

Since the planes have both aesthetic and functional ramifications, the two objectives must be dealt with concurrently in the design process. Thus, when a designer is considering the location of a fence, he must not only be thinking about the size of the volume it will circumscribe and its outward appearance, but

3·21 Linear space.

3·22 Free space.

3·23 An intimate space secured by the low tree canopy.

also, and at the same time, about its relation to wind direction and details regarding its construction and maintenance.

The wisdom underlying the concurrent handling of aesthetics and function is further supported by the fact that aesthetically conceived spaces can serve to make functions more efficient. For instance, static spaces aid in maintaining solitude for passive forms of recreation which would otherwise be destroyed by outside distractions. Static qualities also help the functioning of activities complete unto themselves where inward attention is desired, assisting the concentration of participants as in lawn bowling or assisting the concentration of spectators as in an amphitheater.

Spatial types can also give information suggestive of an action to take. Static spaces provide a logical climax to a journey. The complete nature of the space halts the eye, dashes the urgency to continue forward, and provides the security of knowing that one has arrived. As demonstrated in Fig. 3.20, the static space, therefore, says "Stop." The linear space as shown in Fig. 3.21 says "Go" and thus becomes a logical container for a roadway, bridle path, walkway, etc. The free space as illustrated in Fig. 3.22 suggests "Meander." Here the eye has many choices of direction. It is allowed to wander and frolic. Although free space is therefore unsuited to a function where explicit movement direction is required, it serves quite nicely for unregimented play activities where one can do as he pleases, where he is being encouraged to be in charge and chart his own course.

It is as difficult to think in terms of outdoor volumes as it is to convey their emotional effects if you are not being subjected to them at the same time such a discussion occurs. Communication here is also hampered by the fact that the materials which lay up outdoor spaces are far less obvious than those with which a building architect works, and there are many subtle variations whose form often escapes all but the searching eye. For example, in instances where opaque vertical planes are missing, the simple lowering of a tree canopy creates an intimate *sense* of enclosure. (See Fig. 3.23.) While lacking the sides you would imagine a container to possess, this is still for all essential purposes a space. Its form may not be consciously seen, except perhaps by a student of such things, but it is surely felt by those within.

Whether or not you can trace out an explicit form is secondary to the degree to which you can feel the space's sensation. However, to reinforce the substance of this chapter in your mind, you may wish to seek out both. Accordingly, in any number of outdoor circumstances in which you find yourself, observe what materials go to make up the overhead, vertical, and base planes. Although comprised of earth and plants, you may find that the spaces are as hard and as defined as you have noticed them to be in architecture and can be readily categorized as purely static, linear, or free. Or they may possess merely approximate form, which, if accompanied by sensation, serves their aesthetic purposes as well as those of more obvious definition.

Appraise the impact of the sensations. Sit under the low-hanging branches of a crab apple tree in an enclosed courtyard (Fig. 3.23). It is comfortable for retreat, meditation, subdued conversation? Then place your chair in the middle of a football field or, even better, the Bonneville Salt Flats if it is handy (Fig. 3.24). Feel any difference? Now walk down a road flanked by Lombardy poplars (Fig. 3.25). Are you compelled to move forward? Afterwards, stroll into a flattened wheat field (Fig. 3.26). Have you now lost the urgency to strike out in a definite direction? Finally, survey a panorama of rolling valleys laced with undulating brows of mature trees. Does a refreshing and uplifting feeling come upon you as your eye meanders through the animated volumes? Move down into the nearest glen. Are the initial sensations retained?

This gets us to another point. Just as the functional areas of the site must be considered one in relation to another, so too must the spatial experiences provided. Nobody is plopped into a space from above like a chess piece. He moves through it. Thus, the impact of one space prior to coming upon another must be considered, which means that what the designer strives for is a carefully conceived complex, a sequential organization of related views and sensations. Unless spaces are so connected, much of their impact can be lost in the intervening gaps. The fact that they are disconnected is another reason why many outdoor spaces go unnoticed.

These awareness tests should make it easier for you to understand why a site development plan cannot be adequately appraised as a two-dimensional pattern similar to the flat paper upon which it might be presented. In the critic's eye, the site should leap from the paper as an interlocking sequence of volumes, each space serving a function, each outside room convey-

3·24 *The unrestricted overhead plane denies a sense of comfort to the space.*

3·25 *Strong vertical planes provide a message of movement to the eye.*

3·26 *Lack of vertical definition creates mental ambivalence.*

ing an emotional message, for this is the reality of the plan once it is built. (Compare Fig. 3.27 with Fig. 3.28.)

In the appraisal, however, remember that the full experience will not come from the quality of the spaces alone. As significant as their impact might be, the spatial planes form but the aesthetic skeleton of the site plan. They are only bare walls which remain to be adorned with lines, forms, textures, and colors. It is the grand sum of *all* the emotion-producing elements which produces the experience: effects radiating from enveloping space *coupled with* the characteristics of the lines, forms, textures, and colors found upon the planes and the objects suspended within the space. Substantial experience comes from this complementary type of contribution. Without enclosure, the effects of lines, forms, textures, and colors are watered down. But without the aesthetic elements, the spatial compartments will tend toward sterility.

3·27 *A two-dimensional reading of a site plan is misleading.*

PRINCIPLE 5: ESTABLISH AN APPROPRIATE EXPERIENCE

While order may be advanced through the provision of a dominant effect, it is not ensured unless the effect can be sensed as being appropriate. Stated in another way, it is not enough to simply receive an impact and know what it is. The answer to the question "Why is it?" must also be apparent.

Toward supplying the answer, one design purpose is to provide an experience which extends something the viewer already understands. Such a provision accommodates order by drawing upon a person's tendency to associate one thing as being logical with another: hotdogs and beans, Babe Ruth and baseball, but certainly not ice cream and sauerkraut, Charles de Gaulle and humility.

In site development, surmising that what exists is already understood and therefore accepted, the landscape architect strives to transfer the aesthetic qualities of that which is already present to that which he proposes for new construction. As will be discussed, the existing qualities from which the designer draws his clues of association may be something about the physical character of the site, the personal makeup of the user, or the atmosphere commonly associated with the function. If the landscape architect were to ignore such clues, he would stand the

3·28 *The plan must be interpreted in terms of its three-dimensional reality.*

3·29 *The man-made element is made to grow out of its surroundings.*

3·30 *The man-made element is sited so as to extend the drama of the existing topography.*

3·31 *Nature's textures are repeated in the material of the man-made structure.*

chance of producing a blatant sore thumb. The beholder then would not only be disinclined to embrace it, but because he could not understand "why," would be quite likely to cast it up to ridicule.

This in no way rules out the unique. Indeed, it has been stated that variety and new experiences are essential to everyone's well-being. This does suggest, however, that that which is foreign to past experiences may be more readily accepted, hence more meaningful, if it is rooted in something else which is also familiar. This is quite in keeping with the point regarding dominance. To repeat from a previous page: "While there might be contrasting qualities interspersed for variety's sake, they should occur in restrained amounts so as to remain subservient to the one emotional feeling which has been allowed to dominate." In addition, while this principle is addressed to the provision of order, it will be shown that in its own ambivalent way, its application can also ensure variety.

Matters of Concern

5A. Suited to Personality of Place   Locations have personalities or pervasive moods which can be described as awesome, exhilerating, virile, peaceful, etc. Where these dominant effects are created by nature, everything contributes to the experience. Little hangs out of place. When man interjects his things amidst this order, there is disruption. But the fact that man-made inclusions are concrete, steel, and tailored beams hardly constitutes a license to dismember the prevailing influence. Rather, here is the opportunity, indeed the demand in the interest of buffeting chaos, to continue that which already is by wedding man's works to existing conditions. This is actually common sense, for it is easier to provide a substantial experience through an intensification of what already exists than to first water down a pervasive mood and then begin all over again with the insertion of a feeling created from scratch.

There are two basic ways in which man-made inclusions may be made compatible with their place. The first may be called *physical extension.* That is, new features can be positioned so as to appear to grow organically from the site. Structures may either be tucked into existing corners as indicated in Fig. 3.29 or made to rise from crests as illustrated in Fig. 3.30. The former is a rather passive acknowledgment of prevailing mood, whereas, through exaggeration, the latter accents and hence intensifies an existing emphasis.

The second method works through an *awareness of the factors which give the place its personality:* our old friends, lines, forms, textures, and colors. As found in existing vegetation, soil, minerals, etc., these qualities may be repeated in the construction materials that go into the new. Or dominant forms such as the horizontal sweep of the prairie or the sharp angles of mountain peaks can be reflected in related man-made structures.

This concern is as applicable to natural areas as it is to urban situations, for in both cases it boils down to a desire to achieve transition from the existing to the proposed. In the woods or wherever human structures are quantitatively minimal, the thrust is to make man's works appear to be a part of their natural surroundings. Thus, where nature predominates as shown in Fig. 3.31, the call is: *Blend man with nature.* Wherever buildings and pavements are abundant, there remains no less an opportunity to make developments compatible with the old, for lines, forms, textures, and colors of surrounding structures can readily be reflected in the details of the new works. Or the new may be made to become organic extensions of what exists by the creation of viewing channels to significant features outside the construction limits. Thereby, one is tied to another, making both seem related parts of a whole. Where man is responsible for both the existing and the proposed as illustrated in Fig. 3.32, the parallel call might therefore be: *Blend the new with the old.*

This urge to effect a transition often directs the selection of locations for certain facilities, for it becomes easy to tuck a facility into the site if the proposed location approximates the form of the new structure. Existing hollows are ideal for amphitheaters; valleys are well suited for roadways; broad flats are perfect for playfields. The matching of function to existing site form also minimizes installation costs, for in effecting the blending of the new with the old, all that is required is minor reshaping. (See Fig. 3.33.)

3·32   The patterns of the old building are reflected in the new.

3·33   New construction can be readily fitted to the form of the land if the original surface is approximate to the desired finished grade (L), whereas extensive disturbance occurs where there is a major disparity between the two surfaces (R).

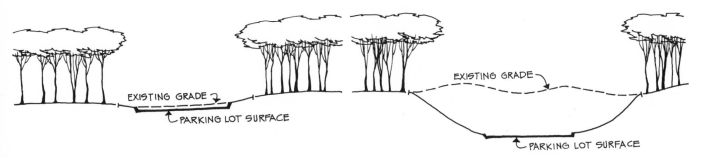

EXISTING GRADE

PARKING LOT SURFACE

EXISTING GRADE

PARKING LOT SURFACE

5B. Suited to Personality of User   In the transition from old to new, creativity can provide certain twists which will ensure that, at the same time, effects which reflect the personality of the user are interjected. This might be called for in private places where individual traits are easy to discern. For an individual of conservative bent, only clean, sharp, no-nonsense design devoid of excessive ornamentation might be desirable since it may be that he is most comfortable within this type of environment. Yet the severity of such design would probably unnerve a more ebullient personality. Such personalizing is well in keeping with the desire to surround a user with familiar matter, for what is dearer to a person than his own self? Success in this can foster a most intensive sense of identity through which may be generated pride.

The premise can be equally well applied to public places (Fig. 3.34) which are used by such definable memberships as ethnic groups or groups with strong regional traits. Flamboyant design seems reasonable for the public squares of the extroverted, and the daring and unorthodox are forms which the pioneer-minded might happily embrace.

5C. Suited to Personality of Function   If we stretch definitions a bit, we will find that activities also have personalities which can be translated into physical development through design. Recognition of such a thesis is useful in situations where the personalities of users cannot be readily determined, for it can be assumed that one has gone to such a place in a frame of mind associated with the anticipated activity. It follows that meditation will be enhanced if it takes place in a peaceful environment (Fig. 3.35), perhaps a static space with cool colors, fine textures, and placid waters, while playground action will be heightened if it is performed in a free space with bright colors and other features which add up to spirited and active surroundings. This placing of function in an expected setting serves to intensify user enjoyment. By aesthetic suggestion, one is encouraged to engage in the activity more fully.

5D. Suited to Scale   Scale is a relative unit of measurement. As expressed in physical features and spaces, its appropriateness must also be sensed in a quality work. Design of outdoor facilities concerns itself with two variations of scale.

The first is *human scale*. To understand his world, man has a tendency to measure things in terms of that with which he is

3·34   *A public plaza.*

3·35   *A place well suited for meditation.*

3·36   *Discomfort: things of human scale are missing.*

most familiar. His most basic "known," hence his most widely used unit of measurement, is his own physical self. Accordingly, if man is to be comfortable, there must be things in space which he can mentally measure in terms of his own height, arm length, width of his finger, etc. If these are not provided as shown in Fig. 3.36, man tends to become confused, for he cannot comprehend. He is overwhelmed. Set yourself in the midst of the vast Grand Canyon and you might be awed. But concurrently you will remain uneasy, for your sense of security will be affected. You will not be able to stand it for any duration. To stem this anguish and gain mental comfort, you need to be surrounded by things of human scale, elements which can be measured in relation to your own self. (See Fig. 3.37.) This holds true for any place where man is expected to linger.

Speed scale is also of design concern, for the swiftness with which you move affects your ability to experience. If you are going at 60 miles per hour in your auto, you can only distinguish the large shapes, sharply contrasting textures, and great masses of color illustrated in Fig. 3.38. Little facets of detail cannot be comprehended.

If you are walking, however, the slower pace enables you to experience the greater intricacy shown in Fig. 3.39. And when you stop, you are able to investigate and understand all textural and color subtleties. In fact, when you sit, you may subconsciously demand such nuances as indicated in Fig. 3.40, for in their absence you may become bored. Here is another example where aesthetic direction is shaped by functional realities. The function, in this case the manner of movement, supplies the purpose behind the aesthetic decision.

UNDERSTANDINGS AND HABITS

The tying of development to place, user, and/or function and the consideration of scale make design visibly logical, for the experience provided is sensed as appropriate. It fits. The preceding can also be used to illustrate other points in retrospect: with attention to these matters, design gains *purpose;* it is addressed to satisfying the senses of *people;* it interweaves both *aesthetics* and *function,* for aesthetic direction is supplied by insights related to how the site will be used. In other words, all the tests posed by the umbrella principles are passed.

3·37   *Security: human scale is present.*

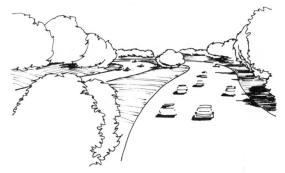
3·38   *While moving at high speed, only masses can be experienced.*

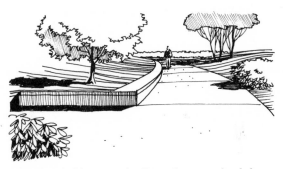
3·39   *At a walking pace, details can be comprehended.*

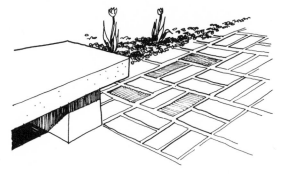
3·40   *When sitting, detail intricacy may be demanded.*

In addition, while instilling order, moves to ensure the appropriateness of experiences, especially those which seek to preserve the existing character of a site, serve variety as well. Just as people vary, so does every land parcel. Like fingerprints, each site is unique. Therefore, measures which are taken to see that the new extends and intensifies present site qualities are steps which will guarantee that the site *remains* unique.

Too many people are blind to this simple device for maintaining what is left of environmental diversity. Those who dump hilltops into valleys or, even worse, obliterate forests with Coney Islands deserve no better than this upon their headstones: "What you have made may be found in many places; but what you have destroyed is found nowhere else in the world."

What might also be carried over from this chapter is awareness of some essential creative purposes. It is the designer's task to place functional areas in appropriate spaces which exist on the site. If such enclosures are only vaguely defined, the landscape architect moves to reinforce their structure so that their experience-producing potential may be realized. Where outdoor rooms of desired type or form do not exist at all, his charge is to create from scratch spaces to serve functions placed within them. Once the spatial skeleton has been so established, the task then is to provide a composition of lines, forms, textures, and colors appropriate for each spatial compartment to finish off the experience.

In addition, toward appraising the relative success of the designer's acts, it would be useful to understand the implications of the aesthetic principles. This should cause you to ask such questions as: Is an experience sensed immediately; does it come on as a definite impression? Is there variety; does the experience remain fresh after many journeys to the site; are new perspectives continually discovered? Give it the second- or third-journey test to ensure that intrigue remains after novelty has worn off.

Is experience appropriate to the function it serves? Or is it completely out of whack with what is going on: a honky-tonk frivolousness in the midst of passive pursuits or placid surroundings for hustle-and-bustle activities? Is there adequate transition between old and new? Is development sensed as an organic extension of its surroundings, or is it a comical sore thumb?

To sharpen your critical abilities so that you may spy the clues which will lead you to ask these and similarly penetrating

3·41 *Rate this scene on your excellence gauge.*

3·42 *Where would you place this vignette on your experience scale?*

questions, pursue some general habits. Compare experiences on your excellence scale. Are they perhaps akin to Figs. 3.41 and 3.42? Negative or weak experience means that the designer has not done his job, whereas positive experience is evidence of the landscape architect's ability to provide refreshment of the mind.

Look at things in aesthetic terms or in terms of the qualities that add up to experience. See that shrubs have texture as well as fences, pavements, earth, etc. Note that a mass of trees can form defining vertical planes just as readily as building walls. Decide for yourself about the sensory potential of three-dimensional volumes in the outdoors.

Search out these qualities. The creation of awareness and the development of critical sensitivity is what this chapter is all about, along with emphasis upon the fact that aesthetics have purpose. These judgments are not frosting-on-the-cake afterthoughts. Ask: Why this color? Why this texture? Why that particular three-dimensional configuration? Why that opening in the space? Why such complete enclosure? Expect clear, logical, and convincing answers.

chapter four

The Functional Considerations

*U*nlike Whistler's art, landscape architecture must be used as well as experienced. Its beauty is irrelevant if its function fails. Functional efficiency can be judged almost entirely on the weight of tangible evidence, for in contrast to aesthetics, where much qualitative analysis depends upon sensing the feel of the thing, the functional effect of design action is predictable. You can focus upon an issue of workability—say, the movement of autos from point A to point B—put yourself in the place of the user, maintenance man, administrator, or whoever else is going to be affected by the issue's ability to perform, and go through all the possible motions of use to determine the functional reasonableness of the scheme.

What is best or highest quality is a product which has no weaknesses. While there should be no letup in pursuing this goal, its achievement may not always be possible. Weaknesses can stem from the unavoidable inability to satisfy conflicting requirements: a demand for a certain provision, but a budget unable to stand the expense; the need for a football field, but a site brimming with precipitous topography. Compromises may have to be found; the critic must be able to distinguish these from questionable conclusions which have resulted from either mental laziness or lack of problem-solving ability on the part of the designer.

The knack which can enable you so to distinguish springs from a continually growing knowledge of what is possible. Thus, it is suggested that you constantly compare park developments and the workability of their parts toward developing a functional kind of *excellence scale* to go along with the aesthetic measuring device already discussed. Extreme cases will be easy to ferret out: it works, or it cannot be used at all; it's the right size, or it is obviously too small for its purposes. As useful tools in determining degrees of quality, the following issues deserve concentration. While each job will have its unique problems, these are the issues generally faced in all instances. As common matters to which solutions must be found, these are the major points which a critic must chase down to conclusion in order to determine the presence of functional quality.

PRINCIPLE 6: SATISFY TECHNICAL REQUIREMENTS

Let's start with the most elementary matters faced in design and therefore those whose handling is the easiest to observe on the site or drawing paper. These are the minimal standards of quantity, structure, and performance which must be met if the product is to be at all usable.

Matters of Concern

6A. Sizes We have said that it makes sense to locate facilities on portions of the site where only slight remodeling of the topography will be necessary to complete the construction. This, along with the self-evident need to ensure adequate elbow room for the functions to be served, requires that the landscape architect test proposed locations against use-area sizes before he can proceed to satisfy more complex requirements. Size information comes from many sources including manuals developed by park agencies, university extension services, and research recreators. The sampling shown in Appendixes 1, 4, and 5 should give you an idea of the kinds of data which are available, while more extensive lists are found in many of the references cited in the bibliography.

Size recommendations for playing fields and court-game areas can be accepted with little question, for such measurements are determined by the rules of the game. However, size suggestions for many common use areas such as totlots and picnic areas can be modified as design purpose might require, for they are fragilely based upon precedents.

For instance, a widely used standard indicates that a totlot should have 2,400 to 5,000 square feet of surface. This has been arrived at by averaging out a sampling of lots in several cities across the country. As reasonable as it might prove out to be, its adequacy should always be checked against the type of equipment, mode of circulation, need for buffer, and other demands of the specific lot to be dealt with before its blanket acceptance.

Individual design requirements then becomes an understandable basis for deviating from a "standard size" suggestion. In addition, as will be demonstrated, existing *site characteristics, design moves* which may be employed, and *agency policies* can serve as equally valid reasons for departure. Consider the standard which suggests ten to fifteen picnic sites per acre (4,356 to 3,904 square feet each). If each picnic area is to be placed upon a base which is stabilized with blacktop or gravel or has privacy screening, more areas may be in order. However, if the site is distinguished by erodible soil, canopy trees which will suffer under concentrated foot traffic, or steep slopes susceptible to gullying, fewer picnic areas, if indeed any, would be advisable.

There are several dual-use concepts which lend adequacy to land areas smaller than standards suggest. One is the school-park policy whereby play facilities used by schoolchildren during the day are released to the neighboring public in the afternoons, evenings, weekends, and summers. Since the same land area is used by both school and park patrons, facility duplication is minimized. Thus, 40 acres of dual use, the school-park, does the same job as 60 acres divided between a separate school ground and a separate park. (Design organization which allows a school-park concept to succeed is illustrated in the chapter on plan evaluation.) Agencies can also put the same patch of ground

4·1 *Inadequate spacing between campsites subverts the camping experience.*

to several uses where seasons of play differ; tennis courts can be flooded for winter skating, football fields can revert to softball diamonds in the spring, etc.

Manual standards are therefore looked upon by the designer as guides and points of departure. Whereas some might be relatively inviolate (a tennis court requires 6,000 square feet), others may be modified in accordance with an analysis of the situation at hand. In addition, many use units, such as passive recreation retreats, cannot be standardized. For these, the amount of site best suited to the purpose usually dictates its eventual size. Caution. In considering deviations, understand that arbitrary adjustments can lead to poor quality. Have you ever seen campers jammed elbow to elbow in violation of the standard which proposes four to seven units (10,890–6,223 square feet each) per acre? As seen in Fig. 4.1, the attractiveness of the area which drew the camper in the first place has been wrecked.

In order to determine size adequacy, you might first check proposals against manual suggestions. Where manuals are unclear or where deviations exist, the application of the key word "why" becomes useful. It should precipitate the designer's rationale, which you may accept or reject toward determining the reasonableness of the departure.

6B. Quantities   Each park contains a number of things—use units and physical items within each unit. Judgments regarding the appropriate type and number of units usually evolve from the demand studies mentioned when we discussed the umbrella considerations. Thus, if five tennis courts or one hundred boat slips are called for, it is because it has been determined that the demand for tennis or boating will cause that many to be used constantly. In most cases, such judgments are but best guesses and have to be reevaluated in accordance with actual participation evidence gathered after installation. This is why it is always good practice to provide for expansion of those facilities whose popularity might be expected to increase in a foreseeable time period.

The number of physical elements considered adequate for each park unit is usually obvious, such as two posts, a net, and nearness to a drinking fountain for a public tennis court. A few others have been identified for us in the ubiquitous standards. (See the Appendixes.) As we have pointed out, many standards can be

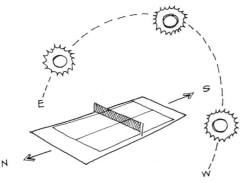

4·2 *Orient tennis courts perpendicular to the sun's course.*

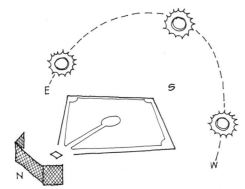

4·3 *Lay out baseball diamonds so that the sun is not in the eyes of the batter.*

4·4 *The sun should be at the back of viewers.*

4·5 *Beaches should receive full solar exposure.*

4·6 *Eastern slopes are ideal for camping where morning dew and afternoon heat are undesirable factors.*

accepted with little question: a family-sized picnic area might very well contain one table, a fireplace, and a trash basket shared by adjacent picnickers; a campground should reasonably have one toilet for every thirty campers. On the other hand, suggesting that the preschool play area should have only the standard chair swings, sandbox, small slide, and simple climbing device may be construed as lazy fabrication.

In evaluating the adequacy of quantities, therefore, attention should be focused upon the count of activity units in relation to anticipated use and the number of physical elements necessary to facilitate that use. But functional quality does not evolve merely from providing adequate room and the proper number of things, as the perpetrators of so many "asphalt jungle" playgrounds and other sterile developments would like us to believe. Even under a self-evident principle such as meeting technical requirements, there are additional matters to square away.

6C. Orientation to Natural Forces   First of all, consider the effects of sun upon activity. To keep blinding rays from participant's eyes, tennis courts and other areas where a ball is sent back and forth in two directions should have their playing axes laid out at a 90-degree angle to the sun's daily course, or essentially a north-south line. (See Fig. 4.2.) For ball diamonds and other facilities where the missile's course cannot be predicted, priorities must be established since all players cannot be given equal protection. Taking baseball for example, a line from the plate through the mound to second base is the axis usually oriented perpendicular to the late afternoon sun (when the sun is lowest, hence its rays most hazardous) since the batter, catcher, and pitcher are in the most immediate zone of precariousness. (See Fig. 4.3.) A similar premise applies where spectators are of primary concern. As shown in Fig. 4.4, a viewing station should be oriented so that the sun remains at the back of visitors during peak hours.

The sun can also be a useful force, and swimming beaches and garden plots should be oriented to either south or west in order to be given the advantage of maximum solar exposure. (See Fig. 4.5.) An eastern orientation is ideal for most campgrounds, for as illustrated in Fig. 4.6, the morning sun can quickly erase overnight dampness, yet its heat is replaced by cooling shade in the afternoon.

Wind is another natural element which can affect activity

efficiency, as is only too obvious to the players who must lean into the gales and chase the frolicking fly balls in San Francisco's Candlestick Park. Ball parks, tennis courts, and other units where missiles are caused to fly about do not belong in the direct course of intensive wind currents. As demonstrated in Fig. 4.7, the direction of wave-billowing winds should also order the location of boat docks. However, wind blockage or lack of atmosphere stirring can hinder camp and picnic ground usability, causing a pall of cooking smoke to continuously hang in the air as if to remind us all of Los Angeles, the ultimate example of inattention to the effects of natural forces in the location of man's works. Therefore, as illustrated in Fig. 4.8, every opportunity should be taken to orient such grounds to the path of available breezes, a criterion which should also be used to determine the placement of other activity areas in heavy humid climes.

The amount of annual rainfall and the periods of drought and downpour present clues as to the seasonal availability of water for wells, fluctuation expectations in the level of water bodies, and flooding possibilities in the lowlands. The absence of underground reservoirs and presence of stream-bank instability and bottomland innundation, or their positive counterparts, can be decisive considerations in locating many facilities.

So, too, can conditions caused by snow, especially when coupled with other matters of orientation. For instance, because of its relation to wind and sunlight, the lee side of a hill and its north-facing slope are where snow loads will be greatest and remain for the longest period of time. Fig. 4.9 therefore suggests the most appropriate location for ski and toboggan runs in temperate zones. It also indicates where the roads which must be kept open in the winter should not be placed.

6D. Operating Needs Appropriately balanced by attention to personal needs, the requirements of cars, boats, maintenance equipment, etc., must claim their share of the planning. The fact that the minimum turning radius of an auto is 20 feet will dictate facets of road and parking lot layout. The knowledge that the maximum grade for a launching ramp is 15 percent indicates what has to be done to the marina bank. The understanding that a power mower cannot negotiate slopes over 33 percent leads to decisions regarding the limits of grassy pitches. Such information as illustrated in Figs. 4.10, 4.11, and 4.12 is gleaned from

4·7   *Boat docks should be located out of the path of water-churning wind.*

4·8   *Picnic areas require breezes to take away cooking smoke.*

4:9   *Heaviest snow loads occur on the lee side of north-facing slopes.*

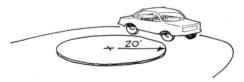

4·10   *Tight turns are hard to negotiate.*

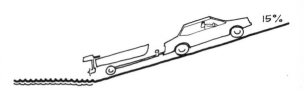

4·11   *Steep pitches are tough to manage.*

4·12   *Drastic slopes are difficult to mow.*

technical manuals and, where these are not available, from measurements taken while the machine is in operation.

As a focus for design concern, "operating needs" can also refer to administrative procedures considered essential to the working efficiency of the recreation complex. This is especially germane to the operation of complicated special use areas such as marinas and zoos where each administrator has strong ideas about how he wants his complex to be run. If the zoo manager considers it most efficient to address his maintenance timetable to those hours when the public is not allowed on the grounds, the designer can opt for a service circulation system which makes generous use of public walkways. However, a network of drives apart from pedestrian ways might be more advisable if heavy service is required during periods of public presence.

Most operational determinations and their effects upon the planning are arrived at through personal interviews between the designer and those who will be running the facility after construction. A cooperative spirit benefits both parties here. Although an understanding of the operator's methods may point one way to efficiency, alternative and possibly more efficient modes of operation might be offered to the administrator by the landscape architect as design possibilities unfold.

Machines and facilities operate. Well, so do people. Their physical limitations must be appreciated in design especially where *comfort* can be affected. As demonstrated in Fig. 4.13, bench design is a serviceable example. Does the edge of the seat catch your leg at mid-calf or mid-thigh, or does seat height allow your knee joint to curve comfortably as God intended? Does the slant of the seat cause your bottom parts to slide unceremoniously into the gap at the base of the back slats? Are the back slats spaced so that each digs into your spinal column? Comfort

4·13 *Bench design must consider the physical limitations of the person.*

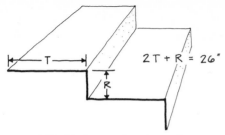

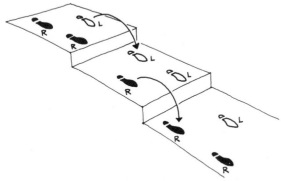

4·14 *Ideal proportions for outdoor steps.*

4·15 *Ramps should allow the user to negotiate the risers with alternate legs.*

4·16 *Consider the comfort of the user in the design of outdoor facilities.*

also decides the question whether to have a back or not to have one. A backless bench may suffice for transient sitting like waiting a few minutes for a bus. But comfortable back support is essential if a long lunch break is anticipated or the *New York Times* is to be read.

How do people walk? In the outdoors, long strides are normal. To maintain a fluid pace, risers for outdoor steps must be comparatively short and trends relatively long. In the interests of walking comfort, landscape architect Thomas Church suggests the following ratio: twice the riser plus the tread equals 26 (Fig. 4.14). Thus, if a riser is 5½ inches, the tread should be 15 inches; where the riser is planned at 6 inches, the tread would be 14 inches, etc. Where more than one foot must be placed on a tread, as in pedestrian ramps, tread length should be designed so that alternative legs can be used in the stepping-up process (Fig. 4.15). To have to step up on the same foot all the time is quite tiring.

Similar insights into the physical operation of the person should also govern fireplace and drinking-fountain heights, as well as point the way to such appreciated conveniences as ramps integrated into stairways for the pushing of baby carriages. (See Fig. 4.16.) Comfort should be a hallmark of every design.

PRINCIPLE 7: MEET NEEDS FOR LOWEST POSSIBLE COST

Although technical needs are rather easy to identify, their satisfaction and those of more illusive requirements often run aground due to a lack of funds to carry out the solution. Here is the most classic conflict faced by the designer for which he must establish a balanced set of priorities—the meeting of needs and, at the same time, costs.

It is incumbent upon the designer to avoid unnecessary costs. He must suggest only what can be supported by sound purpose. Yet, in another sense, he is obliged not to skimp, for his professionalism dictates that his design must satisfy the true needs of the development. The only way out of this dilemma is through a partnership agreement between the client who is footing the bill and the designer who is assuaging his professional conscience. They must *both* determine what are the needs. And they must *together* ensure that such needs are compatible with the monies available to construct the project.

Matters of Concern

7A. Balance of Needs and Budget Such a meeting of the minds begins at the onset of design thinking when an initial program of directives is developed in a brainstorming session between the landscape architect and the owners or administrators of the project. It continues through preliminary stages when the designer comes back to the client with early ideas which might include objectives not apparent at the time of program development, but revealed during periods of design research. And it follows throughout the final stages, when the work is let for bid among contractors and when changes are being contemplated during construction. A proper balance among needs and budget can be most readily struck if budget is discussed at all such gatherings. How much money is available? What are the alternative ways of meeting goals under financial stringencies? What are the high- and low-priority items? What can be constructed in stages to spread out construction costs over a number of years?

In addition to construction funding, the type, extent, and finances of available maintenance will dictate a great deal of what can be done and therefore deserve an important place in the discussion. It is as foolish to consider exotic plantings if expert horticulturists are not on the agency's staff as it is to plan for a public swimming pool if there are no funds available for lengthy upkeep.

During consultations dealing with program, it is usually the responsibility of the designer to draw a full expression of needs out of his client and add to them as his experience suggests. But initiative for identifying needs can come from either party. Regardless of who is the prime contributor in this regard, the key to success of the partnership in the long run is agreement before final design commitments are made. If the trick is turned, each party is forewarned of minimum needs, their relationship to the requirements of budget, and what must be done in the realm of compromise in order to arrange the balance which will turn paper design into reality.

7B. Use of Existing Site Resources It is naïve to suggest that extensive projects can be funded for peanuts. You get what you pay for. But the alert designer takes pains to satisfy needs at only the most necessary of costs. Paramount is the incorporation of existing site resources into his plan. He tries to make best use of what is already there.

The main thrust here has already been presented in "1B. Relation of Use Areas to Site"; that is, facilities should be assigned only to portions of the site which are compatible with that use. Continual emphasis is placed upon this concern because it is so often the key factor underlying the success or failure of land-use projects. Implications span from the most obvious—camping can be disappointing if engaged in upon a poorly drained soil and expensive to accommodate if the land must be underdrained—to the less apparent—conifers (especially pines) die quickly under concentrated foot traffic, whereas such notable hardwoods as hickories and sycamores withstand such concentrations relatively well. Hence, certain species must be ruled out in the accommodation of high-impact uses, while others are reasonable candidates, well suited to that purpose. (See related tables in the Appendixes.)

We have also said that use areas should be placed upon portions of the site which, in their unimproved states, approximate the desired finish grade: football fields in the existing flats, toboggan runs on the available north-facing slopes, etc. In the doing, two concerns are satisfied. It minimizes the cost of earth moving and simplifies the blending of the new with the old. Not only does such attention to function and aesthetics in the same move support the contention that neither can be separated in design thinking, but it also suggests that the inclusion of aesthetic considerations does not necessarily mean greater expense. Indeed, in this instance, money can be saved.

A similar case can be made for locating roadways in available linear spaces where such volumes are formed primarily by earth forms. (See Fig. 4.17.) Since such spaces are usually part of the site's natural drainage pattern, both the aesthetic advantages of enclosure and the functional benefits of eliminating expensive drainage channeling are gained. As shown in Fig. 4.18 this is decidedly true where buildings and major use areas have been located on high ground. Following the drainage network of the site, rainwater is thereby encouraged to continue its natural course, running away from the buildings down the slopes into the roadways, and thence off the site. The site, not the bulldozer

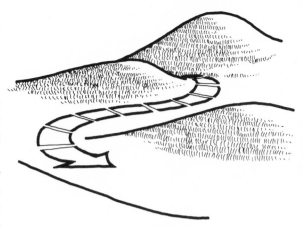

4·17 *Valley floors are natural drainageways.*

4·18 *Roadways placed in the valleys readily take away water draining from use areas located at higher elevations.*

and the expense it brings, has done most of the work for you.

Consider other possibilities to check construction costs. How about using existing buildings to offset the raising of new structures? Rennovate the barn into a maintenance facility or put it to use as an arts and crafts center. Slap some paint on the tool shed and allow it to serve as a control for the tennis court battery. What can be done to eliminate the expense of special footings? See that structures are kept off unstable soil and are placed upon naturally solid bases. Why not eliminate the cost of tree removal and the expense of new plantings? Wrap design forms around existing trees. Place facilities where desired grade already exists so as to minimize the possibility of bulldozer damage. Put facilities enhanced by plantings where plants already exist; place open expanse facilities in spaces uninhabited by tree groves. Remember that it will take at least fifteen years for a newly planted sapling to produce substantial shade and effect, whereas the existing tree might already be of adequate size. How can you ease the financial burden imposed by the construction of lengthy gas, water, electrical, and sewage lines? Locate heavy utility users near existing trunk lines or, in the cases of sewage and water, adjacent to soil suitable for disposal or drilling, thus cutting down the length of feeder pipes and cables.

These and similar measures, taking advantage of what already exists, are decided upon in the design stage of development. After design, the advantages are lost. There is usually little excuse for such loss except downright nearsightedness. And that's only a short step from incompetence.

7C. Provision of Appropriate Structural Materials Often, expenses purposefully added to initial construction costs can amortize themselves many times over through savings in later maintenance. Conversely, skimping on the construction budget can increase eventual costs through the creation of maintenance problems. Considering that the money for both construction and maintenance comes out of the same pocket, such long-run viewing is behind many design suggestions which might appear somewhat extravagant at first glance.

This is quite often true in the selection of building materials. For the base plane, an appropriate selection evolves from an analysis of the type and extent of proposed usage. For instance, the designer should be able to determine where the traffic patterns will be. If these potential paths are not surfaced, the result will be mud, creating visual dishevelment and making the area unusable following rainstorms. There are two solution alternatives. Occasionally disguise the pig wallow with gravel pitched from a wheelbarrow, chart the expense on the maintenance ledger, and watch it exceed the initial costs of a permanent pavement. Or, put down the permanent pavement to begin with and busy your maintenance personnel elsewhere.

After the nature of use has been predicted, the next step is to select a material which can withstand the rigors of the expected activity. A material is happily matched to its use if it passes the following tests:

Durability. Will it stand up under the anticipated pounding?

Appearance. Is it visually compatible with nearby elements?

Availability. It is economically foolish to haul material from distant sources if comparable material is locally handy.

Tactile Qualities. Its feel is especially important where the material will come in contact with the skin as is the case with sitting and playground surfaces.

Climatic Adaptability. Will the material remain stable under such rigors as freezing, thawing, and intense sunlight?

Drainability. Does it allow rainwater to percolate through or run off rapidly and render the area usable after storms?

There are a host of materials to choose from: concrete, brick, cobbles, asphalt, wood blocks, gravel, sand, grass, Astroturf, etc., with many varieties of each. When one is selected in a match with use, the above criteria should be applied with whatever priorities are suggested by the activity; for example, in a playground, you might consider concrete for a peripheral walkway since durability is the most essential criterion and place sand under the swings where softness and quick drainage are of paramount concern. (See Fig. 4.19.) Or, in a neighborhood picnic ground, you might decide on grass for the unpatterned playfield, gravel on the paths connecting each picnic unit, and a concrete pad under each picnic table and fireplace station.

Base-plane problems continually occur where grass is the selected treatment. Grass does well only where it is left untrampled or can be given a chance to recover from the beating it receives from traffic. Thus, if movement is anticipated in a constant line from A to B or is concentrated upon defined square

4·19   Surface treatments related to use: soft and drainable under the play piece; durable where constant foot traffic is expected.

footage, e.g., the immediate vicinity of a picnic table, grass quickly gives way to mud and weeds. One solution to this problem is to move the tables periodically. If this is impractical, base-plane materials other than grass are mandatory. These might range from hard pavements to wood chips or other organic mulch. While the mulch requires periodic replacement, unlike grass, it does not demand spraying, fertilizing, and mowing. On the other hand, grass might be quite appropriate where use is intermittent or the movement from A to B follows several courses with no single pattern predominating.

On the vertical plane, weathering is the primary culprit creating maintenance problems for fences, walls, and building facades. To minimize continuing expense, it would therefore be wise to select materials which need little attention in order to withstand the bombardment of wind, rain, and sunlight. This might mean rust-resistant metals for fittings and fastenings, and stone, brick, and concrete in lieu of wood.

Where wood is used, tinted stains provide a finish which needs only an occasional refreshing, whereas paint demands recoating at more frequent intervals. In addition, the knocking about that occurs in any public place guarantees that painted surfaces will be chipped and flaking long before recoating takes place. However, under the same punishment, stained planes will do no more than slowly fade, thereby preserving a reasonable appearance until restaining can be accomplished. In this regard, depending upon the expense associated with its availability, redwood is the ideal material, for it not only requires no finishing, but is actually enhanced by weathering; wind, rain, and sun turn its unfinished surface to a soft grey after a few years of exposure.

7D. Provision of Appropriate Plant Materials Later expenses attributed to maintenance can also be minimized by the selection of proper plant materials at the time of design decision. Judgments regarding the selection of plants ensue from a recognition of both similarities and differences in relation to other materials. Like lumber, stone, concrete, and other inanimate materials, animate plants can serve to define static and directional spaces, provide human scale detail, screen wind, sun, and views, abate noise, control erosion, and channel circulation. Accordingly, plants like the other materials must be of such size, shape, and staying power as will suit the job they are given. (See Figs. 4.20 through 4.27.)

But plants have unique credentials which set them apart from inanimate elements. Their seasonal changes lend year-round variety which cannot be imitated by nonliving objects which remain first and always as they were set in place. The same plant can be green of leaf in the summer, gold in the fall, laden with berries, branching intricacies, and twig color in the winter, and a kaleidoscope of bloom in the spring.

Further distinguishing plants from other materials is the fact that, as living things, they must be maintained similarly to the way we treat our bodies; which is quite different from the manner in which we keep up our houses. Plants are individuals in that each species requires certain and specific environmental conditions for survival. These demands fall into categories of *soil* (heavy, light, acid, alkaline), *moisture* (constant drinker, seldom thirsty), *exposure* (tolerance to sun, shade, wind), *hardiness* (ability to withstand extreme temperatures). If a plant requires one condition, it will suffer under the opposite. Thus, species which thrive in a swamp will perish if placed in the desert.

In addition, plants can be cataloged as to *life span, susceptibility to certain diseases and pests,* and *ability to survive surface compaction and fill.* Information about the species' places in these categories can deter the selection of elm where the Dutch elm disease is rampant, Lombardy poplar where more than fifteen years life expectancy is desired, or beech where soil must be heaped about the base. If these clues about the plant's life style are disregarded, countless hours must be spent assisting the plant in its fight against its environmental enemies. And, even with such help, the species may not make it.

Therefore, why not try to avoid all but the minimum amount of fertilizing, watering, cultivating, spraying, and wrapping with burlap to ward off the winter winds by planting only those species which appreciate the conditions found on the site. Let nature do most of the work for you. You can't beat her prices.

To take advantage of Mother Nature's maintenance service, a useful rule of thumb might be: If the site is full of growth, select for the new inclusions only those species which normally fit into the "community" of plants in evidence. Under natural conditions, plants survive by swapping needs with other; the

4·20 *Plants can form spaces.*

4·21 *Plants can direct circulation.*

4·22 *Plants can provide detail interest.*

4·23 *Plants can deter wind.*

sun-loving reach above the rest, shadowing the shade-loving, etc. Those who do not contribute to this cooperative arrangement are soon eliminated. To thrust a foreigner among an existing community is to maximize the risks of its survival. This rule has its aesthetic benefits as well, for to put like among like aids in maintaining the prevailing effect.

In the city, where development interferes with growth in natural communities, plants should still be selected in a match with existing albeit artificial conditions. In addition to criteria already stated, such urban considerations as tolerance to *air pollution*, *salt spray* from icy streets, and *pavement reflection* must direct the selection of city plants. Pavement presents a double problem. Besides throwing sun glare in the face of species, it prohibits rainwater from reaching roots. It is therefore unwise to pave right up to major trees, and, if this is unavoidable, the pavement nearest the tree should be perforated or bricked with wide sand joints. The installation expense can be well justified by future savings in maintenance or replacement of dead stock.

Toward the minimization of maintenance chores, the most obvious criteria should also order the selection of plant material. That is, first of all, *plants grow*. Plants should be chosen which have growth habits which naturally fit the circumstances into which they will be placed. (See Fig. 4.28.) This will eliminate the extensive pruning required to hold a plant to atypical form. In days gone by, horticultural fanciers received an immeasurable charge from viewing plants shaped into globes, triangles, and various forms of animal life. Taste aside, perhaps they could afford the grooming effort. With today's burgeoning costs, however, it should be recommended that if one wants to spot a petrified chicken in the park, he should consult a taxidermist rather than a plantsman.

Along with habit, rate of growth and ultimate size should also be considered. The thinking here cuts two ways. If the selection is slow growing, do you have enough patience to wait for it to fill its appointed place? Yet, if it grows too rapidly, how soon before it devours the utility lines or lifts the roof overhang from its joists? To avoid having to wait years for appreciable effect as in the former case, or decapitate major limbs as will be required in the latter, it is wise to select a species which will grow at a pace suited to the circumstances—slow if its corner in the

4·24 *Plants can supply shade.*

4·25 *Plants can buffer odors.*

4·26 *Plants can suffocate noise.*

4·27 *Plants can retard erosion.*

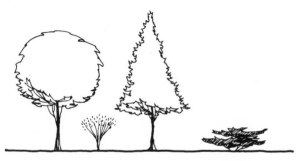

4·28 *Plants have predictable forms.*

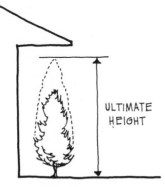

ULTIMATE HEIGHT

4·29 *Plants have predictable growth rates and sizes.*

4·30 *Without undergrowth to take over when the older generation of trees die, the life of this picnic site is limited.*

scheme is cramped and naught but minor pruning is desired to keep it in check; fast growing if it must throw up quick screening—and fit its alloted space upon maturity. (See Fig. 4.29.)

Plants also die. Replacement growth must be continually encouraged. An administrative and maintenance policy can be implemented to reach this end whereby picnic and other areas of intensive traffic are retired periodically to enable underbrush to establish itself. As illustrated in Fig. 4.30, a defeating policy would be to wipe out the scrub because "it looks neater." This disregards the reality that the young material, however disheveled in its infant state, is the best nursery for replacement stock and is already in place. Working themselves to maturity while the taller members decline through old age, the young stock will have reached a point of substantial contribution the day the oldsters expire.

7E. Attention to Details If base-plane materials related to use, vertical-plane materials related to weathering, and plant materials related to location conditions are specified at the time of design, the maintenance budget should breathe a sigh of relief. These are basic matters of concern to which can be added many minor considerations for further savings.

For instance, slopes must be given special attention because they are the ground surfaces most likely to erode. Intensive traffic should be kept away from steep banks inasmuch as constant tromping will obliterate the cover which holds the soil in place. Grassed slopes should be rounded at the tops and bottoms, as if stroked with a butter knife, rather than shaped with abrupt edges, as if hacked out with an axe. As indicated in Fig. 4.31, such rounding provides for both mowing ease and the making of a smooth transition to the surroundings.

While still on the subject of mowing, Fig. 4.32 shows the advantages of paved edging at the base of vertical planes. The mower can cut clean. There is no need to go back with hand clippers to get at the tufts which would have been left by the mower at the base of the wall had the edging not been in place.

Raising planting surfaces (or depressing walks) can deter people from short-cutting through and stomping upon the plants. Similarly depressing sand areas in playgrounds helps to keep the grit in its proper place. Since sand is a fluid material, it will eventually assume a plane parallel to that of the horizon no

4·31 *Smooth slope edges (below) are both practical and visually desirable.*

4·32 *Paving at the base of a wall accommodates one wheel of the mower, thereby leaving a cleanly cut edge.*

matter how it is originally heaped. Therefore, to avoid a slumping overflow, the edges of the container in which the sand is placed should be level.

These are but a few examples of the kinds of details that should be investigated in any design solution. Small in execution, these matters loom large in significance, for they can prevent major maintenance problems.

PRINCIPLE 8: PROVIDE FOR SUPERVISION EASE

Freedom. To be unencumbered by overbearing authority has been suggested as a need common to all people. This immediately appears to conflict with an administrative requirement, the need to have people use the area as intended. Obviously, use must have some supervision. And every public place has its share of legitimate "don'ts." Don't tramp on the flower bed because it will make mud. Don't enter the complex at arbitrary points because this will make it impossible to collect fees. Don't run through the archery range since you may end up with an arrow in your ear.

But "don't" is a culprit word. It nags. It looms as a challenge. In many cases, it defeats purpose because it promotes the misconduct it seeks to put down. What is your normal impulse upon spying a "Keep Off the Grass" sign?

To gain the necessary control, yet retain for the user his sense of freedom, landscape architects attempt to replace "don'ts" with "do's" by organizing use areas and circulation routes in a manner that will make it appear reasonable to use the facility as the designer intends and the administrator desires. This is the easiest way to facilitate supervision—let design layout provide a message which will guide the visitor into a use pattern with which he will agree.

Matters of Concern

8A. Balance of Use Freedom and Control   To what degree *can* control be exercised is a question asked early in the design process. It will be found that there are circumstances in which any attempt to control movement or use is a waste of effort, for the directive will be ignored. The simplest example is where a set pattern of movement cannot be predicted. Where will the user penetrate the large field in order to reach the other side? Unless there is an obvious purpose such as safety served by stepping off at a set point, it will be wherever whim suggests. It becomes folly to demand a single entry point, for the regulation will seem unreasonable. Design should allow whim to take its course. Because it will anyway.

There are also instances where use not only cannot, but *should not*, be regulated. Consider a free play area. To the user, it appears as an arena for doing his own thing. What becomes his attitude, however, when he comes across the signboard which spells out what his thing shall be—and also dictates what it shall not be? Shouldn't there be places not only in every system but also in every park where one can express his individuality, manifest his freedom, satisfy his discovery mechanisms?

Actually, all this proposes to promote is the provision of opportunities formerly available on the late-lamented corner lot. Here was gained a release not possible on sites where there is prescribed only one way of doing things. Here was freedom of choice. Truly free space. The lot is no longer with us. But is that reason to deny the availability of its rewards? Cannot sites or portions of sites be let to simply sit there beckoning the user to wander, dig a hole, build a shack, fly a kite, bake a potato, or rope a calf if he chooses? It's his choice. It's his appetite to be satisfied. It's his needs which the system proposes to serve.

Who can predict every urge? The recreationist conducting demand studies and the behaviorist spinning theories admit to not even being close. As useful as the information provided by these specialists might be, it will never be absolute. How then do you give the unpredictable its due, if not by simply providing a place and letting it happen? Where freedom of movement and intent is deemed desirable, little design elaboration is necessary except in some cases to ensure extensive use flexibility in the structures which are built and the way in which the park units are organized.

This is not to suggest that use discipline should never be required, but to stress that restrictions (or lack of them) be for a purpose. Where it is apparent to all, especially users, that reasonable purposes are being served, conflict between the controlled and the controller is less likely to arise. Thereby, the chances of the directive's being followed are maximized.

8B. Circulation In any public facility which serves great numbers of people, movement is an issue of primary concern. If people can get to where they want to go readily and in doing so not interfere with other activities, peace of mind permeates the site. The charge is therefore before the landscape architect: Anticipate flows. Eliminate obstacles and confusion. Provide unobstructed, well-defined, and logical routes.

Obstacles may be such physical things as boulders and steep topography, but they are more likely to be use areas. It is in the provision of proper relationships among use areas that the designer sets up the first stage of an efficient circulation system. For instance, as diagrammed in Fig. 4.33A, if the parking lot cuts off the picnic area from the swimming beach, it is a cinch that the picnickers will stream through the lot on their way to the water, holding up traffic and endangering lives, no matter how many signs, railings, and other don'ts suggest otherwise. But as shown in Fig. 4.33B, if the parking lot were located peripherally, allowing the picnic grounds to abut the beach, the most direct route would still be followed, only this time with the dangers eliminated.

Similarly, how can you expect kids to keep the noise down in the play space shown in Fig. 4.34A just because it happens to be next to a quiet zone? It is as unreasonable an expectation as anticipating that they will tiptoe through the passive area on their way to the ice-cream wagon. Let's say that a natural barrier of earth and trees is nearby as indicated in Fig. 4.34B. Use it as a buffer. Assign the play space to one side, place the quiet zone on the other, and locate the refreshment stand where access to it from both sides will be unobstructed.

In both examples, the successful relationship patterns suggest do's. The logic of the organization itself tends to supervise the movement, thereby easing the way for the actual linkage of the use areas by roads and walkways. Such linkage, or that aspect of the pattern which is visually evident to you, becomes easy to understand if it is considered as three types of routes: *collector* arteries which connect all major use areas; *secondary* arteries which lead from collectors to connect related spots within a use area; and *minor* arteries which proceed from secondaries to the least-visited facilities.

Working the collector-secondary-minor premise well, a designer can unravel access to a host of activity units in a manner

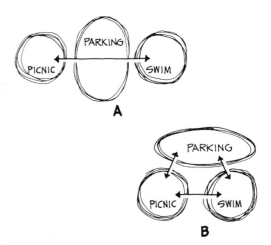

4·33 *Use area organization can encourage either an undesirable (A) or an agreeable (B) traffic flow.*

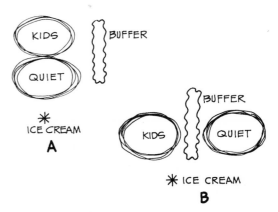

4·34 *A poor relationship system (A) can be eliminated by taking advantage of an existing site characteristic (B).*

which simplifies a traveler's decisions and minimizes his confusion along the way. Firstly, this scheming can eliminate a number of intersections and their accompanying slowdowns from a heavily used collector, for many activity units can be clustered about a single secondary rather than be strung out along the main road, each with its own separate driveway. While all visitors will be using the collector to enter, leave, and search for objectives, only those interested in a related group of activities need be on a secondary. Accordingly, travelers do not have to plow through activity-group X in search of group Y, for each has been segregated out of the main flow. (Compare Fig. 4.35 with Fig. 4.36.)

Confusion is further lessened if each road unit is made to flow smoothly, for people have a tendency to follow consistency in alignment. This would minimize inadvertent movements from collectors to secondaries or minors and the subsequent need to scatter back in search of the artery upon which the journey can be continued. The principle can be applied just as successfully in the reverse. The temptation to move down fire and service roads from which the public is excluded is dashed when such arteries are made to connect with the public way at right angles or otherwise break from the main road's continuity.

The ways in which turns are treated can often mean the difference between free sailing and eternal congestion. Turns should never be made more acute than 90 degrees because at each intersection a decision is being made and the accompanying hesitation, if coupled with a turn difficult to negotiate, could cause a traffic tie-up. In addition, each intersection should be cleared of visual obstacles so that a good view of oncoming travelers can be gained before a move against them is made.

Classic tie-ups are also usual where left-hand turns across traffic are required. Hence, turnoffs should be handled with right-hand movements wherever possible. This is of particular significance for the "entering sequence," for it is upon entering that the traveler, unaccustomed to the layout and searching for objectives, is most confused. A series of left-hand turns, going against the normal right-hand grain that most of us possess and snaking across vehicles speeding from the opposite direction, only adds to that confusion. However, left-hand turns are comparatively inconsequential in the exiting procedure, for by then the traveler has a better feel of the layout, and his quest has been narrowed down to a single objective, the exit.

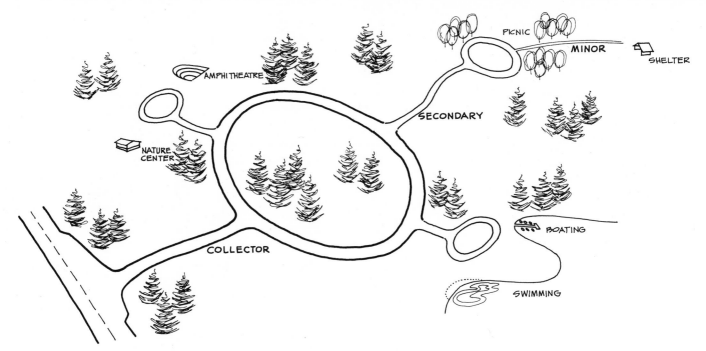

4·35 *An efficient circulation system is distinguished by well-defined routes and consistencies in alignments.*

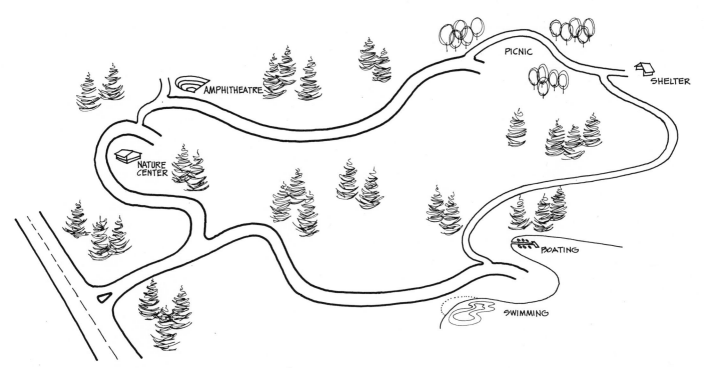

4·36 *Erratic alignments and the separation of related use areas by major arteries are hallmarks of a poor circulation system.*

To help the visitor adapt to an unavoidably confusing layout, points of orientation might be inserted in the development. These could be outstanding pieces of architecture (Fig. 4.37) or natural features which the scheme would cause to continually pop into view regardless of where the user was on the site. Points of orientation are handy references enabling the visitor to know where he is at all times: north, south, east, or west of them; close to, distant from, in front of, or in back of something frequently in view. These references are especially useful in such areas as a zoo or fair where there are so many facilities to visit that the possibilities of becoming spun around and lost are high.

What many of these devices and patterns are actually doing is giving information to the traveler, suggesting to him: Go this way. Go that way. You can find your parked car over there. Etc. The purposeful insertion of abrupt change also provides information, for it can give the traveler cautionary notice that his attention will soon be required. Such changes as dramatic movement from linear to static space, light to dark, human to super-human scale, smooth pavement to rough, etc., snap the mind, thereby creating alertness when approaching potential danger such as an automobile crossing. (See Fig. 4.38.)

Another kind of change which subconsciously informs is the modification of elevation. A slight change such as a curb suggests "keep off." Unlike the "don't" of a sign, this type of suggestion should breed cooperation. Because it is an effort to mount the curb, the traveler will most likely agree to remain in the depression. Where the requirement is mandatory, the vertical can be increased in height in order to say "keep out" in a stronger voice. The ultimate directive is reached when the vertical is elevated above eye level, the barrier in front of the eyes leaving no doubt as to the intent of the circulation pattern.

Out of intelligent use relationships, a simplified collector-secondary-minor artery system, and such detail provisions as negotiable turns, right-hand movements upon entering and at other points of vehicular conflict, adequate sight distance at corners, minimal intersections, points of orientation, and change comes positive information rather than admonishment, guiding the user without creating an overbearing feeling of regimentation. These and related design moves strive toward minimizing signs and such supervisory personnel as the traffic cop on every corner. Design proposes to do the bulk of the work in their stead.

4·37 A significant physical feature may serve as a point of reference where circulation directions are confusing.

4·38 Concrete "rumble strips" warn of an approaching intersection.

8C. Safety Design can also minimize the number of supervisors needed to ensure the safe pursuit of activities. And where such personnel are required, design can ease their chores.

The need for supervision can be lessened by reducing the dangers associated with activity. Many physical hazards can be eliminated by attention once more to use-area relationships. For example, consider tot or casual areas where users, absorbed in benign pursuits, are oblivious to potential harm from other sources. Since their guard is down, they need extra protection from possible collisions caused by spillovers from adjacent areas. It follows that informal spots should be located away from or be well buffered from active areas which might produce the spillover. In addition, sport fields and the like should be oriented so that errant missiles, such as baseballs and frisbees, will not fly into the midst of those whose mental guard is down. The most obvious measures to do away with hazards should also be taken; such blind obstacles as drainage grates in the middle of ballfields should never be allowed.

4·39 Slides, walls, and other play features can be designed for safety without minimizing their challenge potential.

We have said that the challenge of danger may at times be a part of the experience and should not be eliminated altogether. In such cases, design attention to both challenge and security should be balanced as demonstrated in Fig. 4.39. In the playground, walls to traverse might be raised high enough to provide the thrill, yet remain low enough to avoid falls of bone-jarring proportions, and cushioning surfaces (related to use) can be placed in the potential fall zone. Slides can be incorporated into natural slopes so that falls become tumbles rather than the straight-down variety you buy along with the iron-rung piece.

In high-risk areas where supervision is unquestionably called for, whether it be by parents or those on the payroll, design should focus upon the location of visual stations and related sight angles. Use relationships again play an important role. Similar facilities, for example a series of spaces used by tots, need but a single station if organized into a cluster. 360-degree vision is highly possible. If, however, such areas are scattered about the site, stations would be needed for each space since there would be no one spot from which all could be seen.

Besides unobstructed visibility, physical proximity is desirable. Where physical immediacy is not possible, priorities which identify where proximity will be of most value will suggest where the station should go. For instance, if a child who has slipped in

4·40   A parental station should be located outside of the play zone yet remain within view of the children.

the wading pool is plucked quickly, no damage is done. But there is little one can do to avoid injury to the same child once he begins to fall from the top of a climbing device. If it can't be next to both, the station in this case, while within view of the climber, should be adjacent to the pool.

Since design is for people, the supervisor's comfort as well as his ability to perform duties should be taken into account. The relative location of the station should keep him within view of but away from the actual lines of play lest he suffer the inconvenience of being trampled. Details count a lot: shade, wind screening, and the like. And as illustrated in Fig. 4.40, a low barrier between mother and sand pile is always appreciated, for it keeps the grit from her shoes and out of her pocket novel.

8D. Discouraging Undesirables   The problems of hard-core vandalism and perversion are extraordinarily complex matters for which there have yet to appear universally pat answers. In the search for root causes and solutions, parks sometimes serve as places for testing sociological and psychological theories and the release of pent-up maladjustments and injustices. Significant along these lines are the works of a few social-action–oriented designers who have coordinated self-help projects in ghettos where residents and gangs have devised and constructed their own recreation areas on vacant land with locally available materials. One purpose behind this is to spark pride through achievement, thereby combating deep-seated frustrations. The status of such projects is presently in limbo, held up by both the scarcity of designers who care to operate in the unorthodox fashion required and the closed-door policies of some militant factions.

A related and very real concern of park administrators is the need to curb disruption caused by vandals and sexual perverts. Development layout and detailing can either assist or hinder in this regard.

For discussion purposes, vandalism has two sides, although in actual cases, the lines are most likely to be blurred, requiring control measures addressed to both categories. Relatively benign is the nuisance or "push over the outhouse for kicks" type of property destruction. Face it, folks. You did this, too. It is reasonable to assume that much of this damage is caused by people whose basic respect for property is momentarily put aside by a devilish spasm. A development which is neat and in good repair at all times plays upon that respect. It appears worth cherishing and, as such, is less likely to be violated than something which is beat up and broken apart to begin with. The latter invites further destruction.

By way of analogy, consider your new automobile. You take pains to keep from placing the first scratch upon it. But once the first dent appears, the second does not seem to matter as much. And after the third or fourth, the car becomes in your mind just another beat up old "bomb" not worth worrying about. A park inviting this state of disdain becomes equally fair game.

But the park which does not have the first scratch upon it is likely to be cared for, the respect it engenders in many cases squelching the momentary urge to cause damage. Accordingly, the development should be designed for easy maintenance so that with a minimum of effort, especially when that first scratch appears, it can quickly be put back into shape. The use of stains in lieu of paints, the provision of appropriate surfacing where circulation will logically occur, and attention to such details as mowing strips are measures already mentioned in this regard.

The seemingly insolvable problems are in the hard-core habitually vandalized areas where the public's entrenched hang-ups outweigh a basic respect for property. Where these cases are rampant, developments should first of all be designed for sweeping police inspection: potentially vandalized structures clustered rather than distantly spaced about the site; views cleared from the street into the park; if fenced, a minimum number of entry points located within visual range of well-traveled arteries.

To fence or not to fence is a subject of argument among law enforcers. Some feel that fences with controlled gateways sufficiently discourage entrants bent upon destruction. Others maintain that fences impede capture; in the inevitable chase, the younger vandal vaulting fences with élan too often eludes the out-of-shape pursuer still struggling hand-over-hand up the barrier. They reason that the lack of a barrier equalizes the condition of the chase, perhaps giving an edge to the policeman who can drive into the park at any peripheral point and move at will over hill and dale without leaving his cruiser.

The structures themselves, whether they be buildings, signs, picnic tables, fireplaces, or drinking fountains should be sturdy, remembering that the fewer the moving parts, the less chance of their being moved into the creek or someone's garage. A problem which must be recognized in design remains, however. How do you provide sturdy structures that appear reasonably attractive, or at least humane? (See Fig. 4.41.)

Plants should also be given a built-in chance to ward off the voracious appetites of vandals. Some say, specify species with thorns; they can at least fight back. However, they also bring lawsuits and can gouge the innocent. A more reasonable, although not always successful, approach would be to box young transplants with fencing until they have grown to a size sufficient to recover from a beating. In addition, it has been noticed that individual specimens are always the first to go, whereas trees grown in clumps remain surprisingly free from destruction.

Many of the measures suggested to thwart vandals, such as opening the park to sweeping views, are equally applicable to discouraging deviants who would lurk to frighten or attack the unwary. Opening the park to view not only assists police inspection, it bares the act to the passing public as well, which might make the psychopath think twice before manifesting his illness. Within the park, elimination of hidden corners caused by walls, building alcoves, and understory plantings and the supply of adequate night lighting are also useful.

Of greatest attraction to marauders is the empty park and the lone person; of greatest discouragement is the park full of people. Moves toward the latter can come from design; an experience-laden, efficiently functioning development should attract more attendance than a run-down, poorly organized facility. But the primary move comes from the park system planner and the recreation programmer. To keep the park alive with people, it should be located where a real need exists and slated with activities of high public appeal. Concurrently, specialty and introspective pursuits can be allotted to areas which undesirables are less likely to frequent.

UNDERSTANDING AND HABITS

Generation of awareness underlies this chapter as well as the previous block on aesthetics. As with aesthetics, you are urged to establish degrees of workability on an excellence scale for whatever aspects of size and quantitative adequacy, orientation to natural forces, operational demands of machines, people, and procedures, budget, materials, details, use freedom and

4·41 *Sturdy yet attractive park furniture.*

control, circulation, safety, vandal-pervert proofing, etc., come to your attention.

From this habit will spring knowledge which will help you rate your own parks, identify their needs, and give you some idea of how these needs might be satisfied. This is not to say that many of the clever schemes which you find work in one park will solve the problems of another. What knowledge through awareness will certainly do, however, is provide you with enough understanding of how design can satisfy demands per se so that you can judge the relative worth of any design solution proposed to meet your unique needs.

It should be obvious by now that there are many factors to consider in binding requirements into a workable design whole. Up to now, these have been presented in a somewhat scattergun fashion which may have left you groping amid a jungle of considerations, several of which appear to be at odds with each other. Certainly, if our discussions are to help you develop an ability to analyze an intricate solution, a more organized framework for considering these issues must be developed.

In addition, while the principles and matters of concern have been held out as design substance or the critical issues which count toward the success or failure of most proposals, they are but categories and quite general at that. To be useful in evaluating a particular project, they must be made specific or be translated into issues which are uniquely relevant to the project at hand.

After a slight pause to discuss the mechanics of plan presentation, these will be matters attended to next. First will be offered a process which designers use to organize their own minds, for they too need some systematic method for ferreting significance out of a jumble of possible determinants. Design process will then be used as a model which, with a few twists, will be converted into critic's procedure: a thought method which should turn generalities into specifics and allow you to strike at the heart of the design matter while keeping the loose ends tidy as you proceed.

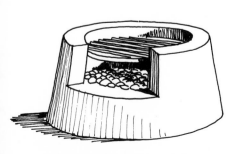
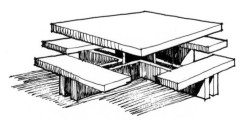

chapter five

Plan Interpretation

*B*efore we proceed to the process for plan creation, we should discuss the plan itself and the symbols which have to be interpreted in order to grasp its meaning. Actually, there are several types of plans with which you should become familiar.

PLAN TYPES

There is first of all the "master plan" (Fig. 5.1) which shows the essential organization of the park including commitments regarding circulation and major relationships: park to surroundings, use areas to site, use areas to use areas, and major structures to use areas. You will find that most documents specifically labeled "master plan" are for extensive developments devouring hundreds of acres or more and are drawn at a scale of $1'' = 100'$ or $1'' = 200'$, the large scales enabling the entire layout to be seen on one sheet but limiting what can be shown to the most general. Even though design decisions are broad stroke at these scales, they still reflect much of the landscape architect's thinking about the blending of the new with the old, area sizes and quantities, orientation to natural forces, and use of existing site resources, in addition to the commitments previously mentioned. What a large-scale master plan lacks is a full representation of proposed lines, forms, textures, and colors, all but the most major contour adjustments, the location of minor structures like light fixtures and drinking fountains, and the handling of other details too small to be drawn in.

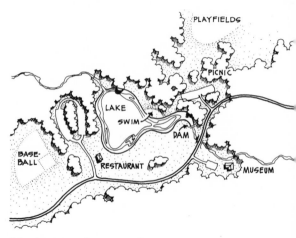

5·1   A portion of a master plan.

These more explicit matters are left to be indicated on the "site plan" (Fig. 5.2) drawn at 1″ = 20′, 1″ = 40′, etc. In addition to expressing more exactly the kinds of things committed at larger scales, the designer can also show aesthetic character, spatial framework, and the location of many minor structures on this drawing. The site plan can stem from one of two sources: it can be a blowup of a portion of the master plan, or it can serve as the master plan itself when no drawing precedes it. The latter is the usual case if the land area under study comprises about 50 acres or less, its moderate size being suited to a rather detailed solution presentation on one sheet of paper.

Where it is required that every fly speck, including curb widths, sign locations, pavement textures, etc., be shown, a "detail plan" (Fig. 5.3) drawn to a scale of 1″ = 10′ or less is in order. This can be an enlargement of a portion of the site plan or, if the area is quite small (a totlot, bus waiting space, etc.), serve alone as a mini-master plan.

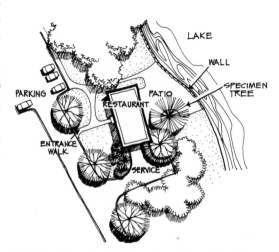

5·2   A portion of a site plan enlarged from Fig. 5·1.

Accompanying each of the above might be "schematic plans" (Fig. 5.4) illustrating circulation patterns, major relationships, or whatever else the designer believes are the keystones of his solution. Schematics are abstracted from the morass of plan detail as a courtesy to the reviewer toward assisting his understanding of the proposal. They are often used as back-up material for verbal presentations or accompany written reports which provide an explanation both of the plan and of the supporting data.

There are other terms by which master, site, and detail plans are known. "Development plan," "master development plan," and, in some loquacious circles, "master site development plan" are a few which come immediately to mind. It is useless to suggest which label goes officially with which plan type inasmuch as there is no general agreement among designers, many using "master plan" when referring to what we have called a site plan, "development plan" for either site or master plan, and an infinite number of other combinations.

What is more important than haggling about titles is understanding what kinds of information each plan type provides, regardless of what the designer you are working with has chosen to call the plan. There are two reasons for this: If you know the degree of design commitment possible at each project scale, you are most likely to put your critical focus on relevant issues rather than waste energies searching for the location of benches on a 1″ = 200′ layout scheme; secondly, knowledge of what each plan can show will allow you to participate in decisions regarding what kinds of drawings are necessary to fulfill your needs.

What we have called a master plan is the first statement of development intent and suggests how all the pieces will fit. With a master plan available, each of its pieces can be built separately with full confidence that, when development is finished, all pieces will knit and work well together. The master drawing is often accompanied by a "staging plan" which indicates how construction might be phased in instances where budget does not permit construction in one financial stroke. The master plan can also be considered a record document showing both the existing and proposed at any given moment. Upon it can be charted changes brought about by new demands occurring in the time span between creation and implementation. The full view of the project provided by the master plan allows the side effects of such changes to become immediately known, pointing out among the interrelated parts of the complex all the measures required to retain the original fit.

What we have termed the site plan gets us closer to construction, for the scale at which it is drawn allows the designer to pinpoint locations and draw up rather precise forms. The site plan, often accompanied by detail plans of some of its parts, provides the basis for "construction plans" (Fig. 5.5) which show measurements, material specifications, structural diagrams, and all the computations needed by contractors to build the works. It is also a guide for the "planting plan" (Fig. 5.6) which is a type of construction drawing indicating to plantsmen where specified plant material is to be installed.

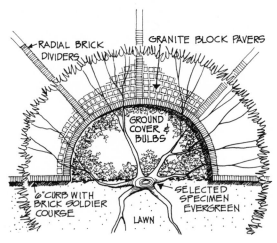

5·3 *A portion of a detail plan blown up from Fig. 5·2.*

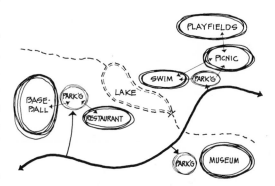

5·4 *A schematic plan simplified from Fig. 5·1.*

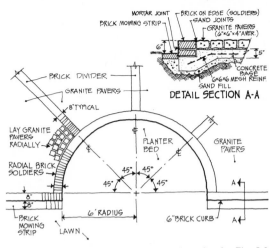

DETAIL SECTION A-A

5·5 A construction plan for Fig. 5·3.

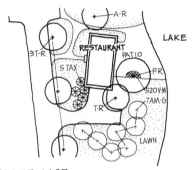

PLANT LIST

SYMBOL	NAME	SIZE	QUANTITY
A-R	Acer rubrum (RED MAPLE)	2½" CAL. B.B.	15
P-R	Pinus resinosa (RED PINE)	Specimen	1
TAX	Taxus cuspidata nana (NANA YEW)	24"-30" B.B.	5
T-R	Tilia redmond (REDMOND LINDEN)	4" CAL. B.B.	4
V-M	Vinca minor (PERIWINKLE)	2'4" POTS	520

5·6 A planting plan for Fig. 5·2.

All of these plans are quite interrelated, one laying the groundwork for the next. Their natures also point out that there are two woven yet distinct phases involved in seeing a job through to construction. The first is the stage of *ideas*, expressed in the master, site, and detail plans. These are the primary talking documents, discussed and modified a number of times before agreement is reached between client and designer. It is only after the ideas are agreed upon that the designer can turn to the next or *working drawing* phase, the construction and planting plans. Most nonprofessionals lack the technical background necessary to accomplish an in-depth review of the working drawings which will be turned over to contractors. Thus, it is during the earlier phase that your chief opportunity to participate as a critic occurs. Fortunately, this is a crucial period, for decisions reached at the idea level dictate most of what will be done in the working drawing phase.

AIDS TO EXPLAINING PLANS

A plan drawing is the usual manner in which a site design solution is presented because its preparation is the least time-consuming among the devices available to illustrate solution essentials. Unfortunately, it is a difficult document for the unschooled reader to comprehend, for while it is shown as a two-dimensional drawing, its reality is three-dimensional. A scale model is a useful alternative. But unlike a plan, a model cannot be reproduced to provide copies to the many who desire its information. It is also expensive to construct, which usually resigns a client to accepting a plan along with the mental gymnastics required for its understanding.

To help a reviewer visualize the plan, the landscape architect often provides various types of sketches illustrating portions of the solution. These may be "elevations," flat representations of objects seen on selected vertical planes (Fig. 5.7); "sections," slices through horizontal planes showing the goings-on above and below ground level (Fig. 5.8); "eye-level perspectives," three-dimensional sketches drawn as people might experience the development from chosen vantage points (Fig. 5.9); or "bird's-eye perspectives," overall three-dimensional views of the development as it might be seen from the upper story of an adjacent building (Fig. 5.10).

5·7 *An elevation.*

5·8 *A section.*

5·9 *An eye-level perspective.*

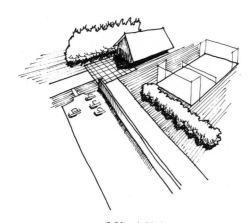

5·10 *A birds-eye perspective.*

While all these aid in putting the plan's message across, they can only show selected aspects of the solution. Even a comprehensive bird's-eye sketch has its shortcomings, for you cannot see behind and underneath many of its elements. Accordingly, the plan itself must be relied upon for answers to most questions concerning its reasonableness.

PLAN EXPRESSION

By drawing with a variety of line weights and colors, the designer attempts to endow a plan with several illusions in order to ease the reviewer's interpretive chore. (Refer to plan drawings in Chapters 6 and 7.) In this regard, a successful drawing is one that appears uncomplicated no matter how much information it includes. This is brought about by setting down visually important objects with heavy strokes and elements of lesser impact with progressively lighter marks. Hence, those objects which define space or form the skeleton of the plan—canopy trees, buildings, etc.—would be made to pop out, with the other elements—pavement patterns, curblines, etc.—receding to the background. Separating out the plan's parts into several levels of visual strength allows each level to be read cleanly, whereas a monotone drawing would serve up the same amount of information as a sheet of unintelligible spaghetti.

The plan should also have a three-dimensional feeling about it to help the reader make the transition in his mind. Edging plan features with shadow marks is a typical technique, but most of the job can be accomplished by the aforementioned line-weight variations. Where the trick is turned well, the plan's parts would read in order of diminishing strength as if you were hovering over the site in a helicopter—which in a sense you are doing when going about your inspection of the drawing. The illusion thus created would also be in line with the actual impact received were you experiencing the plan at eye-level. That is, buildings, trees, and other spatial definers are both those objects which would read strongest on the plan and catch your eye first on the ground. Those elements just under the canopy or second to the buildings in height, small flowering trees, fences, etc., which receive the next heaviest line weight, would also follow the spatial definers in actual visual impact. Grassy patches, cobblestone areas, curblines, etc., would be presented in the lightest line weights, for in reality these would be the last elements to impose their presence upon you.

The symbols drawn on the plan, standing for tangible items which the designer proposes to have installed, can be labeled to explain what they are, but to facilitate interpretation they should also express something of the character we all know the items possess. Thus, the designer might delineate trees as roundish bubbles with ragged edges so that they may be quickly distinguished from buildings drawn with unyielding lines and hard corners. He may symbolize brick with waffle-iron marks so you can immediately judge its extent in relation to the concrete shown on the same plan as a scored sweep and the grass depicted by texture stipples. He may also color his trees purple and cross-hatch his water. Good luck to this dilettante. He's going to have to spend most of his allotted time with you verbally explaining what all those funny looking things on the plan stand for.

CONTOURS

However, there are some strange-appearing things on the plan which cannot be avoided. These are the "contour lines" wiggled over the paper to represent peaks, valleys, slopes—the three-dimensional form of the land surface. (Note following letter references in Fig. 5.11.) Contours are usually drawn as the lightest lines, for in reality they do not exist, being imaginary strokes connecting equal points of elevation on the ground. The term "elevation" stands for a height above or below an assumed plane of reference or datum, the usual datum being sea level which is expressed as elevation 0. Thus, if a contour is labeled 90, the points which it connects are 90 feet above the surface of the sea (A).

On most plans, dashed lines (B) represent the existing contours, while unbroken lines (C) indicate those proposed. However, if only existing contours are shown, they may be entire lines, the usual rule being violated by those labor-conscious designers who feel that unbroken lines can be put down faster than dashes.

Visualization of the land configuration as expressed by contours requires a hard-to-come-by facility, but if the knack is acquired, the greatest problem in seeing the plan in three-dimen-

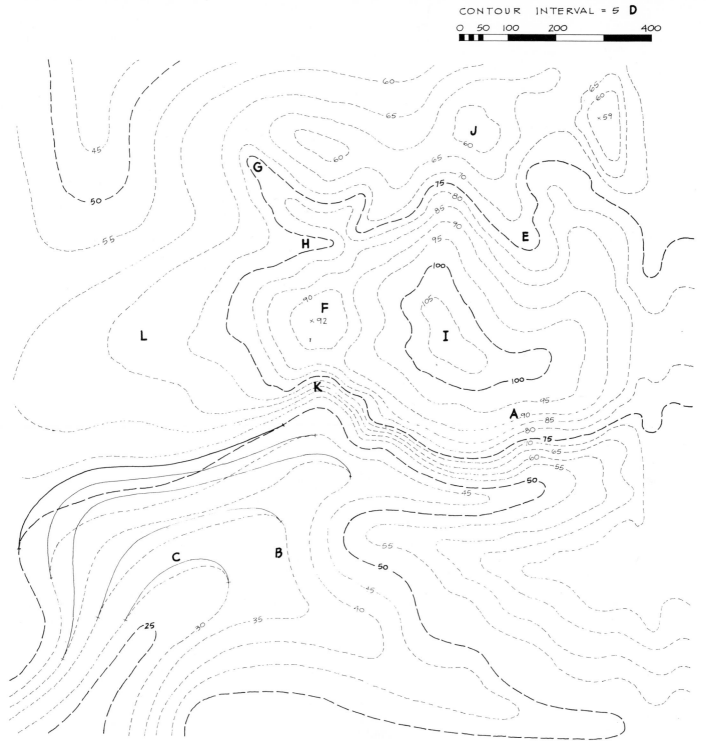

CONTOUR INTERVAL = 5 **D**

0 50 100 200 400

5·11 *A topographic map.*

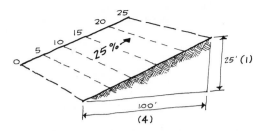

5·12   *The slope of the land can be referred to in terms of a ratio or a percentage.*

sions virtually disappears. Thus, a real effort toward grasping the picture portrayed by these funny lines pays off manyfold.

In reading contour lines, here are a few technicalities you must consider:

1. Every plan has a "contour interval" which remains constant throughout the drawing. The interval is designated in the plan legend (D) and stands for the vertical distance between each line. For readability's sake, every fifth contour is heavied (E). Therefore, if a contour interval is stated as 5 feet, the lines drawn on the plan connect elevations 75, 80, 85, 90, 95—or whatever they might be labeled in increments of five—with lines 75, 100, etc., shown a degree darker than the others.

2. "Spot elevations" such as "×92" are occasionally inserted to indicate critical points lying between the contour lines (F).

3. Bends ("noses") in a contour point either down a ridge (G) or up a valley (H).

4. A closed contour indicates either a summit (I) or a depression (J) in the ground.

5. The closer the contours, the steeper the slope (K); the farther apart the lines, the more gentle the pitch (L).

6. The steepest part of the slope is that which runs perpendicular to the direction of the contour lines.

7. "Gradient" (slope pitch) is usually expressed either as a ratio of horizontal run to vertical rise (for example, 4:1), or a percentage. (A vertical rise of 25 feet per 100 feet of run would be a 25 percent gradient.) (See Fig. 5.12.)

The gradient can be easily computed from a plan where contours are shown. If you wish to know the grade as a ratio, first determine horizontal run by measuring the ground surface distance between several contour lines. This measurement can be taken with either an engineer's scale (marked off in decimals) or an architect's rule (scored in fractions) flipped to the side which represents the scale at which the plan has been drawn. Then multiply the number of contours found in the area of horizontal measurement by the contour interval. This gives you the vertical rise which is divided into the run measurement to arrive at the figures required in the ratio. To determine the grade as a percentage, simply count from the contour lines the number of feet the ground rises in a measured distance of 100 horizontal feet and place a percent symbol after the result.

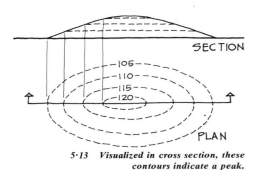

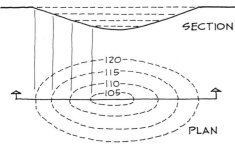

5·13 *Visualized in cross section, these contours indicate a peak.*

5·14 *A cross section shows that these contours depict a depression.*

Certain visualization exercises will help you realize the relative steepness of the slopes represented by these figures and should otherwise give you a feel of the land. Develop the habit of doing cross sections or slices through the plan areas you wish to visualize. Do dozens on paper initially as demonstrated in Figs. 5.13 and 5.14 and soon you will find yourself drawing them automatically in your head everytime you spy a contour map or want to have answered such questions as: Is that a peak or a valley? How rugged are those undulations? How flat is the surface proposed for the ball diamond?

Concurrently, you might run 100-foot measuring tapes out in the hall. Have one end held on the floor, raise the other the number of feet required for the grade percentage you wish to picture. The slope that you will see on the tape surface will be the actual pitch of the ground whose contours compute to the figure you are using.

Begin to check out plans on the site. As you move through the development, picture yourself walking inside the plan. Eventually, the reverse should be true to the point where every time you pick up a plan drawing, you will immediately climb in, walk around, and come away with not only a feeling of the land form, but a three-dimensional impression of all the other design essentials as well.

chapter six
Site Design Process

*T*he ability one needs to design recreation areas is similar to that required to solve any kind of land-use problem, the primary difference between park design and, say, that of a subdivision being the inputs which are analyzed toward solution. Accordingly, you will find that most designers have worked their way into a park design specialty from a general education in landscape architecture, just as you know that doctors receive a basic medical background before turning to brain surgery.

Development of design expertise does not occur overnight, for it takes an inordinate amount of time and patience spent in simply doing: testing, discovering, and prodding latent talents to the surface. Much of the trial, error, and frustration that this entails is due to the fact that no one has yet invented a design cookbook containing procedures which guarantee results if followed. However, what many designers adhere to with some success is a process which helps them sort out the facts, premises, and combinations which lead to solution.

The process aids the landscape architect by systematically focusing his attention on those factors which could affect the design's outcome and otherwise lends a semblance of organization to his attack. By illuminating relevant factors, it also serves to trigger flashes of inspiration. The process therefore assists both the rational and intuitive powers that the designer must call upon in order to satisfy the demands of the project. While the process provides a framework for action, its ultimate value as a design tool is contingent upon the designer's ability to work those powers interchangeably within it.

A systematic approach to site design includes three phases. The first is a "survey" or an assembling of facts and data which might have consequences for the design's outcome. The second is "analysis" or the making of value judgments about the effects of one fact upon another. The third step may be called "synthesis" or the weaving of the results of analysis into a comprehensive form and organization solution to the problem. The steps may not be taken according to the strict chronology discussed here, for there is much feedback and interplay among them. In addition, the process must remain flexible in order to allow each designer to work his mental powers in a way which is most comfortable to him.

SURVEY

Program Development

Each phase has several parts. The first is the preparation of a program expressing the early requirements of the project. Either handed to the landscape architect by the client or its development delegated to the designer if the client does not have the means to shape it up, the program establishes goals to be accomplished. These might be set down as: *tangible items* (10 tennis courts), *capacities* (picnic facilities for 200 people), *physical benefits* (nonabrasive play surfaces), or *intangible gains* (being an educational institution, the school should have grounds which show respect for the natural environment). Agency *policies* whose implementation would depend upon how well the site was developed might also be included (a desire to collect entrance fees), as well as information regarding available *construction and maintenance funds*.

The program gives the designer direction for subsequent steps in his thinking, yet it is always a flexible document, subject to modification as that thinking progresses. This is because not only the answers but many of the questions remain unclear until the end. Additional items might be suggested to take advantage of site potential discovered midway through the analysis phase: a skiing complex offered to exploit the many steep slopes. Capacities may have to be adjusted due to site restrictions: fewer cabins planned to ensure that sewage distribution fields are not overloaded. In some cases, items may have to be eliminated entirely from consideration as being unfeasible: swimming taken from the list because the water is found to be polluted.

As the design process begins to uncover solution possibilities, the program may also be augmented with criteria unique to the job at hand. Many will be spun from those principles and matters of concern found to be most relevant to the project. For instance, in the study of use-area relationships, the designer might realize that day users will be drawn to different attractions than overnight guests and conclude that facilities for the former shoud be organized apart from those associated with the latter. Additional directives might come from research into the technical requirements of the program items.

On counts other than the debated territorial imperative, in large measure the program should reflect the voiced desires of the people whom the park will eventually serve. However, on some sad occasions, this is not the case, the list of facilities to be incorporated being drawn up in a vacuum by either the designer or administrator. This leads to the possibility that the park will include only those things its developers like to do.

The citizenry becomes involved when many of the program items come from demand-study interpretations, the questionnaire route being quite satisfactory for most developments serving the diverse population that would be attracted to either a citywide complex or one located away from population centers. When development is proposed for the neighborhood, however, more direct involvement on the part of the public in program preparation, including continuing face-to-face consultations with the designer, is highly desirable. This is especially significant

TOPOGRAPHY

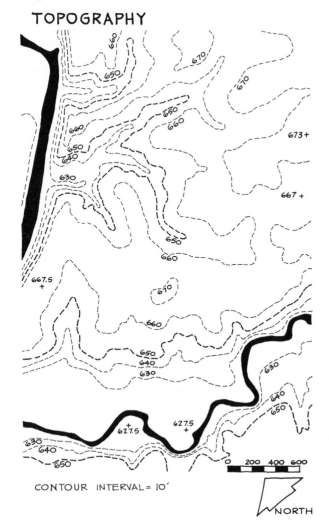

CONTOUR INTERVAL = 10′

6·1 Site data.

SLOPE GRADIENTS

	0-2%
	2-4%
	4-10%
	10-20%
	OVER 20%

6·2 Site data.

DRAINAGE PATTERNS

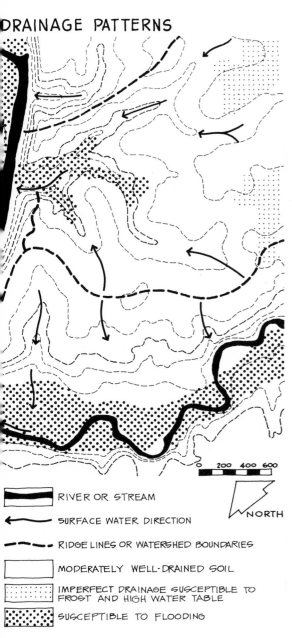

RIVER OR STREAM

SURFACE WATER DIRECTION

RIDGE LINES OR WATERSHED BOUNDARIES

MODERATELY WELL-DRAINED SOIL

IMPERFECT DRAINAGE SUSCEPTIBLE TO FROST AND HIGH WATER TABLE

SUSCEPTIBLE TO FLOODING

0 200 400 600

NORTH

6·3 Site data.

where serving the urban poor to whom the neighborhood is essentially the entire world and a major source of identity. To deny the residents a direct hand in determining what will be theirs, while outsiders ram through what they alone imagine to be cute, is both arrogant and patronizing. It is the stuff from which public alienation is made.

Inventory of On-site Factors

After the program has been thrashed out, the designer turns to gathering facts about the site, securing information from maps and personal inspections of the area under study. Such data could include the location of and/or knowledge about existing:

1. Man-made elements
    a. Legal and physical boundaries, private holdings, and public easements
    b. Buildings, bridges, and other structures including those of historical and archeological significance
    c. Roads, walks, and other transportation ways
    d. Electric lines, gas mains, and other utilities
    e. Land uses: agriculture, industrial, recreation, etc.
    f. Applicable ordinances as zoning regulations, health codes, etc.
2. Natural resources
    a. Topography, including high and low points (Fig. 6.1), gradients (Fig. 6.2), and drainage patterns (Fig. 6.3)
    b. Soil types, by name if available, for clues regarding ground surface permeability, stability, and fertility (Fig. 6.4)
    c. Water bodies, including permanence, fluctuations, and other habits
    d. Subsurface matter: geology of the underlying rock including existence of commercially or functionally valuable material as sand and gravel, coal, water, etc.
    e. Vegetation types (mixed hardwoods, pine forest, prairie grassland, etc.) and individual specimens of consequence (Fig. 6.5)
    f. Wildlife including existence of desirable habitats as low cover for pheasants, caves for bears, berries for birds, etc.
3. Natural forces (including both macroclimate as generally

SOIL TYPES

TIMBER SOILS

[27]
MIAMI LOAM

[107]
SAWMILL SILT CLAY LOAM

233
BIRKBECK SILT LOAM

[236]
REESVILLE SILT LOAM

[322]
RUSSEL SILT LOAM

[451]
LAWSON SILT LOAM

PRAIRIE SOILS

[152]
DRUMMER SILTY CLAY LOAM

MIXED TIMBER AND PRAIRIE SOILS

[234]
SUNBURY SILT LOAM

NORTH

6·4 *Site data.*

found over the entire site and microclimate characteristics or changes from the norm as experienced in isolated patches)

a. Temperature (air and water) especially day, night, and seasonal norms, extremes, and their durations

b. Sun angles at various seasons and times of the day

c. Sun pockets as might be found in such as forest clearings; frost pockets which may be in low places where the wind that sweeps away the morning dew is blocked

d. Wind directions and intensities as they occur daily and seasonally

e. Precipitation: rain, snow, and sleet seasons and accumulations; storm frequencies and intensities

VEGETATION

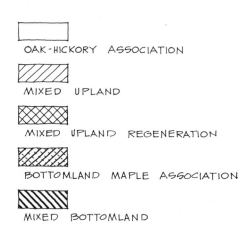

OAK-HICKORY ASSOCIATION

MIXED UPLAND

MIXED UPLAND REGENERATION

BOTTOMLAND MAPLE ASSOCIATION

MIXED BOTTOMLAND

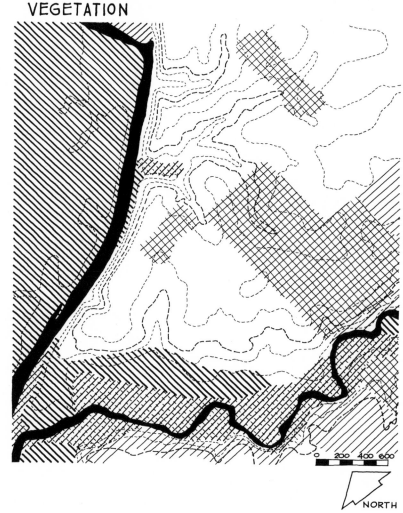

NORTH

6·5 *Site data.*

4. Perceptual characteristics
   a. Views into and out from the site; significant features
   b. Smells and sounds and their sources
   c. Spatial patterns
   d. Lines, forms, textures, and colors and scales which give the site its peculiar character
   e. General impressions regarding experience potential of the site and its parts

Inventory of Off-site Factors

The designer must also accumulate information about the man-made, natural, and perceptual elements on the properties which

PROGRAM

ENTRY CONTROL BUILDING

NATURE CENTER

SERVICE YARD

BOAT REPAIR AREA

NATURE TRAILS

PICNICKING

PLAYFIELD

COMFORT STATION

SWIMMING

MARINA

ROWBOAT & EQUIPMENT
RENTAL BUILDING

PARKING

CONCESSION

BATHHOUSE

6·6 Design process case study.

PROGRAM RELATIONSHIPS

1. NATURE CENTER
   A. TRAILS
   B. PARKING

2. PICNICKING
   A. PLAYFIELDS
   B. COMFORT STATION
   C. CONCESSION
   D. PARKING

3. SWIMMING
   A. BATHHOUSE
   B. CONCESSION
   C. PARKING

4. MARINA
   A. RENTAL BUILDING
   B. BOAT REPAIR
   C. CONCESSION
   D. PARKING

5. SERVICE YARD
   A. ENTRY CONTROL

6·7 Design process case study.

surround or otherwise affect the site. These might include both existing and anticipated:

1. Land-use patterns
2. Stream and drainage sources
3. Visuals, smells, and sounds
4. Neighboring aesthetic character
5. Public utility locations and capacities
6. Transportation ways and systems

Each step in the survey phase begins in isolation, the first facts collected being but those which are immediately handy. Soon all steps become intertwined, each giving direction to another in order to turn general notions of what might be needed into specific requirements and ensure that nothing which could affect the design's outcome has been left out of consideration. The designer finds himself working back and forth between program and inventory. Program items suggest to him not only what information must be collected, but also what is inconsequential. The fact that a playground is being dealt with sends the landscape architect after data about sun angles and the peripheral traffic situation. At the same time, it suggests little urgency to seek out a map showing the location of bear dens and pheasant cover. In a complementary fashion, as we have discussed, data garnered might point out modifications necessary in the program.

To see how this and subsequent phases work, your attention is directed to the accompanying case study which has been simplified so that details will not get in the way of the points to be made. First, note in Fig. 6.6 the program comprised of items which we will assume have been agreed upon as meeting the needs of the park users. Relate the items to the drawing labeled "site analysis" (Fig. 6.9) in order to see what categories of survey information the program has suggested as being worthy of investigation. Then reflect upon the diagrams and drawings in turn as each is explained in the following.

ANALYSIS

Program Relationships (Fig. 6.7)

While data are being collected, design ideas are germinating, but they are held in the back of the designer's mind until he has taken a more comprehensive look at development possibilities. This begins by grouping program items into logical associations in order to understand something about their interdependence.

Relationship Diagrams (Fig. 6.8)

Thoughts about interdependence are then translated into diagrammatic form, the designer investigating how the major units might work well together in plan and how circulation might be facilitated between them. Neither scale nor site information enters the landscape architect's mind at this point; he concentrates solely upon functional relationships and lines of travel. Many combinations will be tried as the landscape architect attempts to work out the bugs of prior diagrams in subsequent ones. Finally, he arrives at a scheme which, in his estimation, expresses an ideal functional pattern for the program's major use areas.

Site Analysis (Fig. 6.9)

Now the designer turns his analytical eye to the site, first compiling the inventory items on a topographic map. Those items which lend themselves to graphic representation—vegetative cover, water, soil, etc.—are expressed in sweeping patterns and color coded according to variety or condition. This is done so that the character of the site can be read at a glance, allowing the designer to quickly spy areas suited for certain of the program items. For instance, land forms might be marked off in four colors: one designating slopes of less than 1 percent where drainage is always a problem; another standing for surfaces of 1 to 3 percent that may be suitable for all types of construction with little or no earth moving; the third indicating areas of 4 to 9 percent grade, the land suited to building and roadway installation with moderate grading; and the fourth showing slopes of 10 percent or greater which will require major site adjustments if built upon. Breakdown increments will vary with each project, depending upon the slope requirements of the program units to be installed.

In addition, natural and perceptual influences—wind directions, noise sources, etc.—are illustrated with bold symbols, and other considerations are set down in note form where they apply on the map. The latter might be directives the designer has issued himself according to the ideas which have been germinating in the back of his mind: "Save rock outcropping." Or,

RELATIONSHIP DIAGRAMS

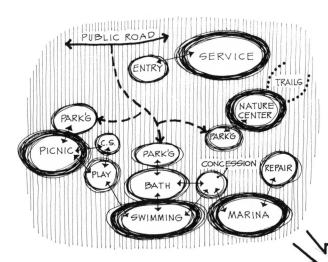

+ ENTRY CONTROL NEAR PUBLIC ROAD.
+ PARKING — SPLIT, DOESN'T PENETRATE ACTIVITIES.
+ ONE CONCESSION FOR SWIMMING & MARINA WHICH SHOULD BOTH BE NEAR WATER.
+ PICNIC & SWIMMING SHARE PLAY FIELD.
− MARINA NOISE & DEBRIS CONFLICT WITH SWIMMING.
− PICNIC DIVORCED FROM NATURE CENTER.
− NATURE CENTER WEDGED BETWEEN NOISY SERVICE AND REPAIR.

+ BATH-CONCESSION COMBINED TO SEPARATE SWIMMING & MARINA.
+ PICNIC & NATURE CENTER PARKING COMBINED.
+ SWIMMING & MARINA PARKING COMBINED.
+ REPAIR & SERVICE (NOISE & MESS) COMBINED.
− PICNICKERS GO THRU N.C. AND TRAILS TO SWIM & BOAT.
− ROADS CUT PICNIC FROM BOATING.

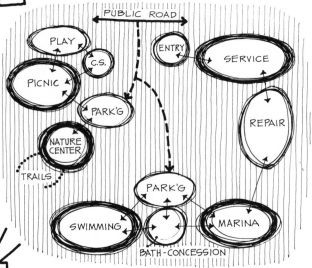

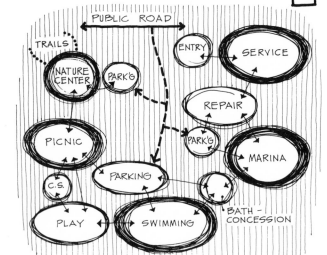

+ PARKING — SPLIT, DOESN'T PENETRATE ACTIVITIES (PEOPLE DON'T CROSS ROADS TO GET TO ANYTHING).
+ N.C. ISOLATED BUT CONVENIENT TO PICNIC AREA WHICH WILL PROVIDE MAJORITY OF VISITORS.
+ BATH-CONCESSION SEPARATE MARINA & SWIMMING.
+ PLAY SEPARATE BUT USABLE BY BOTH SWIMMING AND PICNIC.
+ MARINA, REPAIR & SERVICE TOGETHER — NOISE ISOLATED FROM REST OF PARK.
+ ENTRY CONTROL NEAR PUBLIC ROAD, FIRST CONTACT.

THIS IS IT !

SITE ANALYSIS

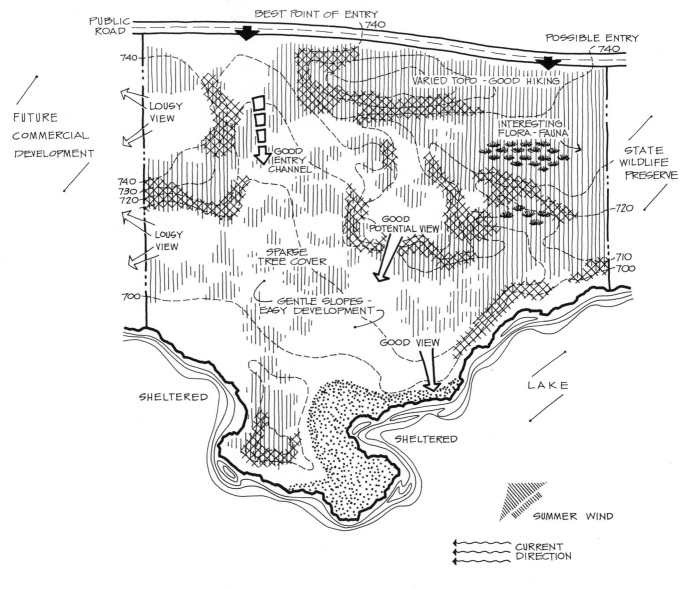

NORTH

PUBLIC ROAD

BEST POINT OF ENTRY

POSSIBLE ENTRY

740

740

740

FUTURE COMMERCIAL DEVELOPMENT

LOUSY VIEW

VARIED TOPO - GOOD HIKING

INTERESTING FLORA - FAUNA

STATE WILDLIFE PRESERVE

740
730
720

720

GOOD ENTRY CHANNEL

LOUSY VIEW

GOOD POTENTIAL VIEW

710
700

700

SPARSE TREE COVER

GENTLE SLOPES - EASY DEVELOPMENT

GOOD VIEW

SHELTERED

LAKE

SHELTERED

SUMMER WIND

CURRENT DIRECTION

LEGEND

(vertical lines)	WOODED AREA
(cross-hatch)	SLOPES EXCEEDING 5%
(marsh symbol)	MARSHY AREA
(dots)	SANDY AREA
――――――	CONTOUR LINE

6·8 (opposite) and 6·9 (above)   Design process case study.

because by now he has a feel for the program requirements, they may be qualitative in nature: "Good place for entrance."

In the analysis phase of the design process, the designer strives to gain a full understanding of program requirements and an intimate knowledge of the limitations and potentials of the site before he begins to make concrete decisions. This phase also serves to flash possibilities for solution in the designer's mind, alternatives founded in the logic of the analyses he is making.

As in the survey phase, analytical steps are first taken singly, but soon swing into a back-and-forth effort, with a growing knowledge of program needs directing the search for particular site qualities, and a rising feeling for the site illuminating what can be done to satisfy the program's demands. Concurrently, research and criteria reevaluations are proceeding so that, when the time comes to put the pieces together, the designer knows full well what tests a successful synthesis must pass.

SYNTHESIS

Design Concept (Fig. 6.10)

Up to now, one issue at a time has been placed in front of the landscape architect in a progression of interrelated complexity. Proceeding in such a fashion, the designer is less likely to be panic-stricken by the magnitude of the problem than if he attempted to address himself to the entirety of the project at the onset.

With a sure handle on required relationships and site influences, he opens the synthesis phase with an attempt to fit the ideal functional diagram to the site. What he reads from the diagram and therefore tries to place upon the ground is its working essence rather than its literal image; that is, a diagrammatic sketch which shows one use unit lying next to another does not demand that one must appear to the right of the other when placed upon the plan. Rather, it offers the more general suggestion that they require adjacency on the site. The designer is therefore free to reverse, shift, rotate, warp, or otherwise manipulate the diagram elements in whatever manner needed to see that all use units end up on desirable portions of the site in a pattern which retains the essential relationships implied in the abstract diagram.

DESIGN CONCEPT

NORTH

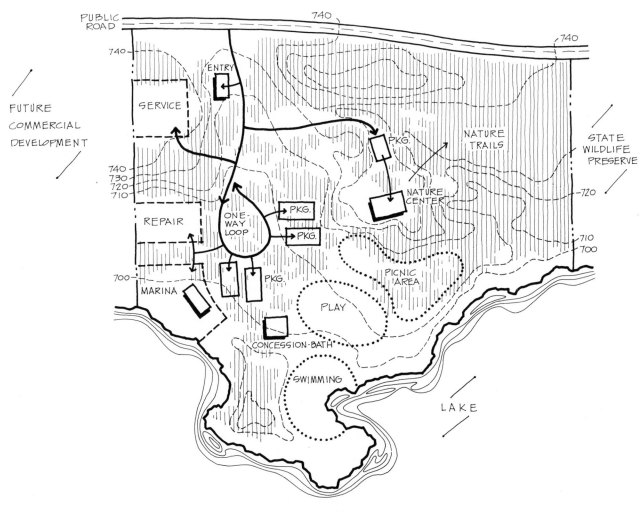

PUBLIC ROAD

740

740

740

FUTURE COMMERCIAL DEVELOPMENT

740
730
720
710

ENTRY

SERVICE

REPAIR

ONE-WAY LOOP

PKG.

PKG.

PKG.

700

MARINA

PKG.

CONCESSION-BATH

PLAY

SWIMMING

PKG.

NATURE CENTER

NATURE TRAILS

STATE WILDLIFE PRESERVE

720

710
700

PICNIC AREA

LAKE

RELATION OF USE AREAS TO SITE

1. NATURE CENTER
- GOOD VIEW
- APPROXIMATE TO DIVERSE NATURAL INTEREST AREA
- ISOLATED BY TOPO FROM OFFENSIVE TRAFFIC & NOISE

2. PICNICKING
- FLAT SITE
- STABLE SOIL
- CANOPY TREES
- VIEW OF WATER, YET AS SAFETY MEASURE, SEPARATED FROM LAKE BY TOPO
- IN PATH OF SUMMER BREEZES FROM LAKE
- RELATED PLAY AREA IN FLAT, TREELESS SPACE

3. SWIMMING
- SANDY SOIL
- SHELTERED COVE
- MAXIMUM SOLAR EXPOSURE

4. MARINA
- SHELTERED
- APPROXIMATE TO COMPATIBLE COMMERCIAL DEVELOPMENT
- FLAT SITE
- STABLE SOIL
- RELATED REPAIR AREA FLAT AND TREELESS, UNAFFECTED BY POOR VIEW

5. SERVICE YARD
- FLAT, CLEARED SITE, UNAFFECTED BY POOR VIEW
- STABLE SOIL
- SEPARATED FROM PUBLIC AREAS BY TOPO

6. ROADS & PARKING LOTS
- FLAT TOPO AVOIDING EXCESSIVE CUT & FILL
- STABLE SOIL
- SPARSE TREES PROVIDE COVER YET ALIGNMENT AVOIDS REMOVAL OF VEGETATION
- EXISTING SPATIAL CHANNELS

6·10 Design process case study.

REFINED PLAN

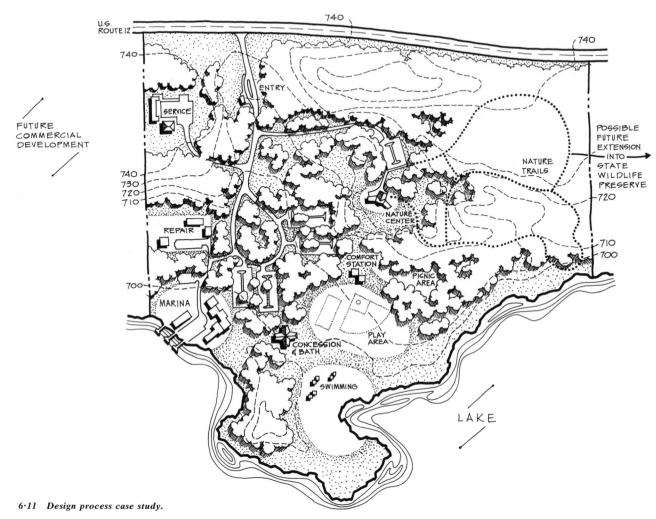

6·11 *Design process case study.*

What takes place in the designer's mind during synthesis is impossible to describe except to say that it entails a series of impulsive reactions to the conditions of the problem as they unfold. In no particular order, save one in which the individual designer feels at ease, he may start by selecting a perfect location for one use area, work circulation to it, then roll the other units from it. He may relocate areas whose initial positioning violates the sense of the relationship diagram or revise the whole to ameliorate the negative effects of the relocation, and then turn to refinements that satisfy a single criterion. As he gathers steam, the designer finds himself reacting to all factors at once, working simultaneously among all the solution aspects until at last the desired whole is visualized.

The product is a skeleton concept, much like an outline for a book, only presented in graphic form. Use units are illustrated in approximate size and form where they belong on the site. Traffic channels are placed where they are expected to be. The spatial structure is set. Additional work remains, for the skeleton must be fleshed with a myriad of details, but these will supplement rather than materially change the major commitments made to this point.

Refined Plan (Fig. 6. 11)

Within the concept framework, the designer proceeds to make precision adjustments, add minor use areas and structures, and do whatever else is necessary to give the solution pattern its finished form.

Final Plan

The work is now drawn up as a "preliminary plan" ready to receive the review of the client. A single refined concept may be presented if the landscape architect feels that the problem can be solved in only one manner. A number of alternatives may be trotted out if the designer has either evolved several equally desirable relationship diagrams or discovered that a single diagram can be fitted to the site in a variety of ways.

During the review session, the designer explains the reasons behind his moves while the client darts a question here and there, mulling over the ideas generated by the drawings. A successful review ends with agreement about the proposal usually contingent upon the incorporation of modifications requested by the client. Back on the drawing board, the revisions are made and the plan is finalized.

chapter seven

Plan Evaluation

Although their chores are different throughout their performances, designers and critics are confronted with many similar situations. Beginning with little understanding of solution direction, both are vulnerable to panic in the face of the project's magnitude and both need a clear view of where to begin. While early feelings of what is needed might be possessed, such generalities must be turned into specific requirements in order to direct attention to the significant determinants of the case. The success of the end product, whether it be plan drawing or evaluation, hinges on the ability to make correct value judgments about the propriety of the synthesis.

The best aid that can be suggested for the critic—as well as for the designer—is a systematic approach that helps sort out determinants, although this cannot guarantee results inasmuch as a favorable outcome depends upon how well the critic operates his mind within the framework provided by the system. While any evaluation procedure is therefore but a tool, the one suggested here should arm the critic with enough understanding of the situation to surround his conclusions with confidence.

SELECTING THE DESIGNER

Ensuring an appropriate solution to your land-use problem begins long before the plan is developed. It starts with the selection of the landscape architect. If he's good at his profession, your critique becomes but a cordial review, lasting just long enough to satisfy your curiosity, leaving ample time in the evening to toast both your fine judgment and his at a parlor of good cheer.

If the designer is an employee of your agency, you already have an idea of his ability by virtue of previously monitored performances. However, many park departments do not budget a full-time design staff, preferring to contract the preparation of each development plan to a private consultant. Selecting a qualified consultant is an art which should be mastered by the financing party to the contract. It involves a searching analysis of the designer's references and past performances. Several candidates should be asked to present their credentials; while one might appear adequate to the task, comparison with the qualifications of others will confirm a decision that the best has been chosen.

There is frequently a tendency to keep the money at home by selecting a designer from the immediate area, but this should be tempered by a desire to choose a consultant who is detached from the pressures of local politics and vested interests. Whether he be from around the area or from out of town, the landscape architect must be able to provide an objective solution to the problem.

Those landscape architectural firms who devote all or portions of their practices to the design of recreation areas should be asked to supply examples of prior works representing tasks similar to the one you wish pursued. Inspect the graphics and accompanying texts and draw conclusions about the depth of analysis and breadth of thought which these chapters have suggested should be expected of a competent designer. During the formal interview, quiz the designer regarding the handling of issues which we have also discussed here.

While specialty experience deserves consideration, don't overlook landscape architects whose practices lack park projects, remembering that their education proposes to equip them with an ability to treat all types of land-use problems. Even the office with the highest concentration of recreation areas under its belt started somewhere. In reviewing samples of their work, look for the handling of design aspects similar to those associated with parks—circulation, use-area relationships, resource utilization, aesthetic experience, etc. Excellence of accomplishment in these categories, and professional presence under the fire of examination, may very well indicate a capacity to meet your specific challenge and provide the quality you seek.

Landscape architects compete for commissions on the basis of ability rather than on the price of their services, for their code of ethics prohibits fee bidding. This is not to suggest that you should avoid negotiating with the designer over both the extent and cost of his work. Determining whether or not you can afford the service is your right as well as a most practical consideration. However, such discussions should be delayed until after you have measured the consultant's competence, for it is upon this that the solution to your problem rests.

PREPARATION

A landscape architect—the type from whom you would not want to buy a used car—once said that he could convince a client to accept anything because, when he presented a proposal, he was the only one prepared. Fortunately, such cavalier attitudes are rare, but the lesson remains: All parties to an issue should be familiar with its parts if they wish to guard their interests when the issue comes up for discussion. To those who have a stake in the quality of a park design proposal, preparation for discussion means the acquisition of at least a feeling for the nature of the problem and some understanding of the factors which could affect its solution.

This can be yours through knowledge of program requirements and site characteristics, the former gleaned from cursory research or by reflecting upon what is in your mind by virtue of personal acquaintance with program activities; for example, you may be an expert equestrian and thus quite knowledgeable about stable development and bridle path layout. Information about the site can be revealed through inspection of a topographic map or an on-the-ground reconnaissance. From these thoughts can evolve a list of factors which you consider important in resolving the problem.

If more thorough preparation fits your mood or the circumstances, you can expand your list of important considerations by setting each of the principles and matters of concern against what you understand about the program and site. When played against the particulars of the problem, the principles and matters of concern act as triggering phrases, dislodging from the back of your mind a host of specific issues which you feel the designer should ponder on his way to solution.

To see how this might work, let's assume that a baseball diamond is required by the program. Baseball is selected because most of you are familiar with the game and need no preceding research in order to participate in this exercise. Check off the following against it, asking yourself what each item brings to mind in terms of design decisions which should be made regarding the diamond's functioning and aesthetic appeal.

1. Everything must have a purpose.
   a. Relation to park to surroundings
   b. Relation of use areas to site
   c. Relation of use areas to use areas
   d. Relation of major structures to use areas
   e. Relation of minor structures to minor structures
2. Design must be for people.
   a. Balance of impersonal and personal needs
3. Both function and aesthetics must be satisfied.
   a. Balance of dollar and human values
4. Establish a substantial experience.
   a. Effects of lines, forms, textures, and colors
   b. Effects of dominance
   c. Effects of enclosure
5. Establish an appropriate experience.
   a. Suited to personality of place
   b. Suited to personality of user
   c. Suited to personality of function
   d. Suited to scale
6. Satisfy technical requirements.
   a. Sizes

b. Quantities
c. Orientation to natural forces
d. Operating needs
7. Meet needs for lowest possible cost.
   a. Balance of needs and budget
   b. Use of existing site resources
   c. Provision of appropriate structural materials
   d. Provision of appropriate plant materials
   e. Attention to details
8. Provide for supervision ease.
   a. Balance of use freedom and control
   b. Circulation
   c. Safety
   d. Discouraging undesirables

Following are some thoughts which these categories might trigger. But don't look at them until you have first gone through the suggested procedure and set down your own ideas. Since your purpose will be to identify thought areas in which design decisions must be made, the form in which they occur to you is inconsequential. They may be stated as directives which should be followed, questions you want answered, specific concerns whose treatment deserves inspection, etc.

As you proceed, you may draw a blank with some matters, but this is to be expected since certain categories will be less applicable than others with a few totally irrelevant to particular facilities. For example, in a complex of amateur sport fields, baseball may have few if any dealings with major structures. But even this negative conclusion has value in preparing for evaluation since the issue has been considered before being thrown out, giving some assurance that an exception to the usual has not been overlooked.

In addition, do not be frustrated if repetitions emerge as you tick off the categories. Double checks have been built into the principles and matters of concern in accordance with the contention that if one way of phrasing does not dislodge a significant thought, perhaps a synonymous one will. That is, if the fact that a baseball diamond needs a flat surface does not dawn upon you when you dwell upon "relation of use areas to site," there is the additional chance of its being brought to mind by "use of existing site resources."

When you have completed this exercise, compare your list against the one provided to see how close you come, or if indeed you have uncovered other factors.

Some Factors Affecting the Design of a Baseball Field

Buffer noise and flight of errant baseballs.

Flat surface draining to periphery.

Direct access from parking lots or pedestrian entrances to spectator area.

Location of drinking fountains, comfort stations, concession stands.

Maintenance equipment stored near diamond or elsewhere?

Positioning of bleachers or other viewing accommodations.

Static space.

Cleared field.

Dark outfield background.

Layout dimensions according to rules of the game including at least 300 feet down each foul line.

Is fee control necessary?

Sun out of eyes of batter and pitcher.

Soil appropriate for grass growth.

Permeable soil.

Avoid access to other park units across outfield.

No hidden obstacles in playing field.

Lighting system on egress routes for twilight games.

Do this for all units in the program. While it may take a bit of time to evolve lists of factors for the first few units, the pace should quicken with subsequent ones as your habits of concentration improve and as you begin to pick up common factors; e.g., areas for lawn bowling and tennis need to be laid out according to the official dimensions of the games just as the baseball diamond is. Checking off the principles and matters of concern against the full body of units in the program should also make you conscious of relationships—lawn bowling and tennis courts should be located away from the baseball field—which should be jotted down as they occur to you.

Not much more than an hour of uninterrupted concentration should be all you'll need to effectively run through most programs regardless of their lengths. It is not necessary to work out solutions to the problems you uncover or decide beyond speculation how determinants might best be handled. This is what the designer is doing for you. Remember also that, while you may see some directions which you think solution might take, they are most likely fragments untied to other considerations. Therefore, you should not carry into critique prejudgments as to what the final form and organization might be, for your thoughts have not been tested among the full range of priorities. Nor is it required that you come up with an all-inclusive list of concerns. In fact, it would be as impossible to derive an all-inclusive analysis of the problem at this stage of contact as it would be for the designer to be able to predict all aspects of the solution while in the middle of analysis.

With these cautions in mind, any information which becomes yours, no matter how cursory or brief, serves the primary purpose of the procedure: orienting you to the nature of the problem so that you will not have to approach the plan drawing cold. By creating awareness of what may be involved, the procedure also sharpens your ability to react to the proposal as it will be presented by the designer.

In addition, you have developed a checklist comprising focus points or items related to the specific project which will demand your attention during critique. They can also be starting points from which an ensuing discussion, allowed to take its course, may direct eyes to other significant matters.

A desire to become oriented and bring specific focus points into being should also motivate your inspection of the site. Warming up for evaluation, such an inspection should work toward discovering as many site limitations and potentials as possible in the time put to the study and according to information you have available.

Your site review may be assisted by the principles and matters of concern, triggering thoughts in a fashion similar to that suggested to help cull information about the program. Or your attention to site determinants might be directed by points on the program checklist. Consider our previous baseball example. The fact that the facility requires a flat surface and permeable soil should send you searching after those characteristics on the site. Your findings are additional focus points, in this case, site potentials and limitations whose management in the solution should be observed. These may be compiled as an addendum to the program checklist or, better yet, jotted down in place on a topographic map of the site. Since the designer will be presenting his conclusions on a map, this should facilitate comparisons.

You should now be quite able to approach the proposed solution *on its own terms*.

CRITIQUE

The opportunity to evaluate may occur in many ways. It may come in the form of a plan routed across your desk. In this case, the plan is unlikely to be accompanied by its designer. Or you may be given a written report outlining the vitals of the proposal to which the plan is attached. You may also be a party to a preliminary plan presentation made personally by the landscape architect. While the following approach supposes that the designer is present, most of the steps fit the other instances as well.

I. *Understand what the designer has done.* During his presentation, make notes when questions come to mind. During the discussion period which usually follows the unveiling, pin down the designer on matters of justification. If you cannot follow his reasoning, ask for clarification. If such things as topographic relief, character of lines, forms, textures, and colors, and the nature of the spatial sequences cannot be read by you from the plan, ask to have them explained. If you feel that something has not been made clear, ask to have it reexplained. If you do not understand the significance of an issue, ask. Ask. Ask. There are no stupid questions. Only questions.

II. *Consider the designer's goals.* These are his primary objectives or criteria which support the major design decisions and should show up in the designer's opening remarks or appear early in his written report. Are they valid?

   A. If you agree that his purposes are advisable, proceed to the next step without qualification.

   B. If you are not entirely convinced by the reasoning underlying some goals, engage in the next step, qualifying subsequent judgments accordingly.

   C. If you feel that the designer's criteria are completely unfounded—they are as muddle-headed as "tree cover should be obliterated inasmuch as it adds nothing to the value of the site"—forget about the next step. Critique only the goals and write off the work as a completely misguided effort.

III. *Evaluate goal realization.* The following should help fix your attention and sum up thoughts during presentation and discussion. It can also be used as a procedure for treating in detail those plans which are available for lengthy study.

A. From the plan, abstract its concept. Do this in your mind or on tracing paper and you will have an uncluttered view of the proposal's functional and aesthetic skeleton: its major use areas, circulation patterns, and spatial structure.

B. Either mentally or physically, overlay this skeleton on a site analysis (perhaps the topographic map upon which you compiled preparatory impressions). Actually, toward fostering understanding of the proposal, a concept abstraction and site analysis should be available to you from the designer as part of his presentation package.

1. Upon these drawings, bring to bear the full force of what you know about design in general and the specific thoughts you have regarding the particular project, treating first the *complex-at-large.* From the schematics, with an occasional allusion to the original drawing, make broad judgments regarding:

   a. Satisfaction of stated goals and additional criteria which you feel are warranted.

   b. Relation of park to surroundings.

   c. Relation to use areas to site.

   d. Relation of use areas to use areas.

   e. Relation of major structures to use areas.

   f. Circulation.

   g. Spatial experiences.

   h. Aesthetic character.

   i. Provisions for order and variety.

2. Now go back to the parent drawing and make more detailed judgments about *each major use area.* Go through the areas in some reasonable chronology: right to left; north to south; as found along the major arteries; passive areas, then active ones; or from day use units to overnight facilities.

   a. Concentrate on the same issues as 1 a–i, above.

b. Apply relevant focus points from your checklist.

3. When that has been accomplished, draw conclusions about *each object found within each use area.* Judgments throughout, but especially here, should consider the degree of design commitment possible at the plan scale and the type of drawing being studied. As we said in the chapter on plan interpretation, the location of light fixtures is not a decision reached at 1"=200'; the naming of plant species is not a requisite of the master plan but belongs on the planting plan, etc.

4. Finally, against what at this stage of inspection should be a comfortable understanding of the solution proposal, go over all the principles and matters of concern in order to see if missing issues remain. Now you are ready to sum up.

CASE STUDIES

Let's try out the procedure. Following are some plans waiting to test your insights. The first (Fig. 7.4) is adapted from an actual professional proposal originally drawn at 1"=50' scale. Evaluation has been made easy for you by virtue of the accompanying program (Fig. 7.1), site analysis (Fig. 7.2), concept schematic (Fig. 7.3), and summary explanation of its strong and weak points. The latter is instructional in nature, giving reasons behind the conclusions and offering further tips on how to approach the drawings. A critique on your part, addressed only to the substance of the plan, need not be as verbose. With this in mind, you may wish to attempt a review of your own before turning to the evaluation supplied and comparing your findings with the ones provided.

The second example (Fig. 7.5) is another solution for the same problem. This was not the consultant's answer, but has been worked up especially for this book to illustrate some errors which could render a proposal useless. Inasmuch as there is no explanation provided, you will have to find the weaknesses yourself, using the same program and site analysis, but abstracting your own version of the concept.

You are entirely on your own for the remaining four studies. These too have been hypothetically created for this book in order to present conditions illustrative of many of the matters we have discussed. While not actual cases, they do typify much of what you might expect when dealing with live circumstances.

These four are presented in pairs. The first two cases (Figs. 7.9 and 7.10) represent comparative solutions to a single problem and were originally drawn at 1″=200′ scale. The final couplet (Figs. 7.13 and 7.14) depicts proposals for a project initially prepared at scale 1″=10′. Each pair is preceded by the related program comprising uses and initial criteria and a topographic map of the site upon which have been placed a few analytical notes transferred from other documents which have not been made available to you (Figs. 7.6, 7.7, 7.8 and Figs. 7.11, 7.12 respectively). Missing is the concept abstraction and evaluation which you must supply.

A SCHOOL PARK   PROGRAM

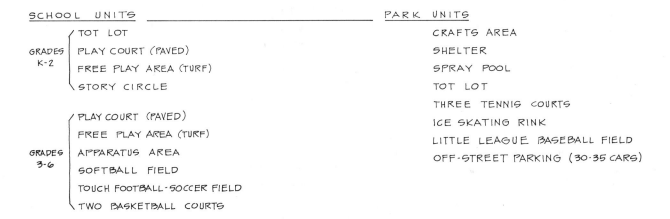

SCHOOL UNITS

GRADES K-2
- TOT LOT
- PLAY COURT (PAVED)
- FREE PLAY AREA (TURF)
- STORY CIRCLE

GRADES 3-6
- PLAY COURT (PAVED)
- FREE PLAY AREA (TURF)
- APPARATUS AREA
- SOFTBALL FIELD
- TOUCH FOOTBALL-SOCCER FIELD
- TWO BASKETBALL COURTS

PARK UNITS
- CRAFTS AREA
- SHELTER
- SPRAY POOL
- TOT LOT
- THREE TENNIS COURTS
- ICE SKATING RINK
- LITTLE LEAGUE BASEBALL FIELD
- OFF-STREET PARKING (30-35 CARS)

CRITERIA

1. ISOLATE SCHOOL FACILITIES FROM PARK UNITS TO MINIMIZE OVERLAP INTERFERENCE DURING SCHOOL HOURS. YET, IN ORDER TO TAKE ADVANTAGE OF THE SCHOOL-PARK CONCEPT (AVOIDS FACILITY DUPLICATION ; REQUIRES LESS LAND THAN COMPLETELY SEPARATE DEVELOPMENTS), ACCOMMODATE A DUAL USE FLOW FOR THOSE PERIODS WHEN SCHOOL IS NOT IN SESSION.

2. PROVIDE EDUCATIONAL EXPERIENCES.

3. RELOCATE EXISTING SERVICE DRIVE TO MINIMIZE HAZARDS OF MIXING KIDS WITH VEHICLES.

4. PROVIDE RELIEF FROM THE LOCAL ENVIRONMENTAL DULLNESS THAT RESULTS FROM THE COMMUNITY BEING SURROUNDED BY ENDLESS FLAT CORNFIELDS.

7·1

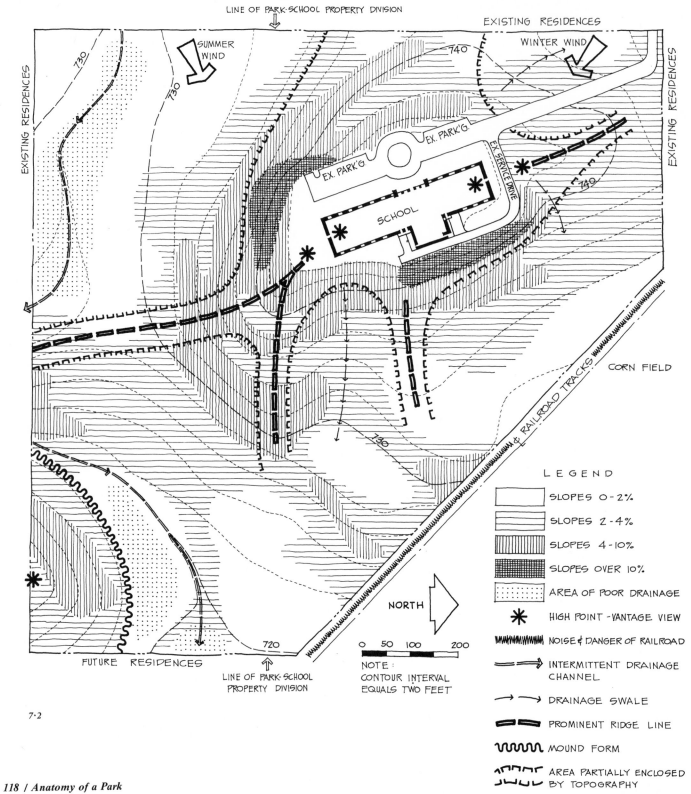

A SCHOOL PARK   SITE ANALYSIS

LINE OF PARK-SCHOOL PROPERTY DIVISION

EXISTING RESIDENCES

SUMMER WIND

WINTER WIND

EXISTING RESIDENCES

EXISTING RESIDENCES

730

730

740

EX. PARK'G

EX. PARK'G

EX. PARK'G

EX. SERVICE DRIVE

SCHOOL

740

730

CORN FIELD

RAILROAD TRACKS

720

FUTURE RESIDENCES

LINE OF PARK-SCHOOL PROPERTY DIVISION

NOTE:
CONTOUR INTERVAL
EQUALS TWO FEET

NORTH

0   50   100   200

LEGEND

SLOPES 0-2%

SLOPES 2-4%

SLOPES 4-10%

SLOPES OVER 10%

AREA OF POOR DRAINAGE

✳ HIGH POINT - VANTAGE VIEW

NOISE & DANGER OF RAILROAD

INTERMITTENT DRAINAGE CHANNEL

DRAINAGE SWALE

PROMINENT RIDGE LINE

MOUND FORM

AREA PARTIALLY ENCLOSED BY TOPOGRAPHY

SOIL: SLOW PERCOLATION RATE

7·2

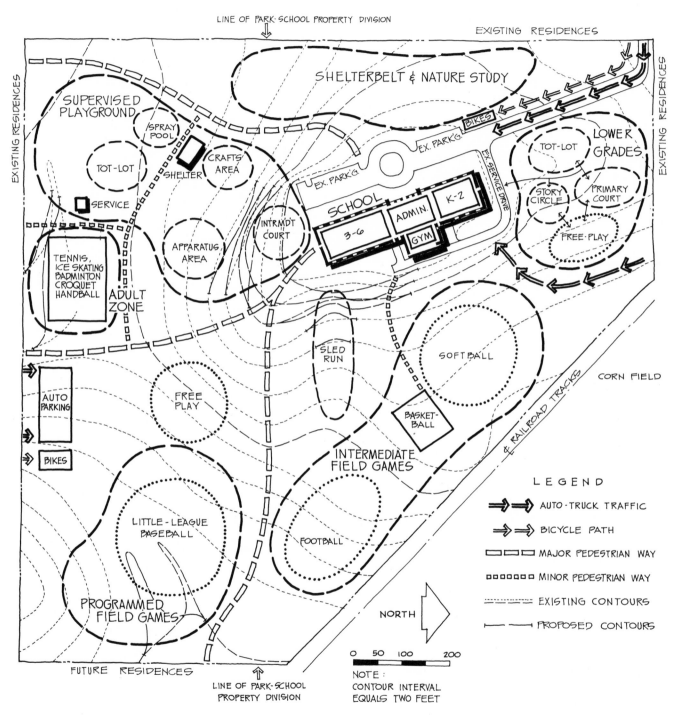

LINE OF PARK-SCHOOL PROPERTY DIVISION

EXISTING RESIDENCES

SHELTERBELT & NATURE STUDY

SUPERVISED PLAYGROUND

SPRAY POOL

TOT-LOT

SHELTER

CRAFTS AREA

SERVICE

APPARATUS AREA

INTRMDT COURT

EX. PARK'G.

BIKES

EX. PARK'G.

EX. PARK'G.

EX. SERVICE DRIVE

TOT-LOT

LOWER GRADES

STORY CIRCLE

PRIMARY COURT

FREE-PLAY

SCHOOL 3-6

ADMIN.

GYM

K-2

TENNIS, ICE SKATING BADMINTON CROQUET HANDBALL

ADULT ZONE

SLED RUN

SOFTBALL

AUTO PARKING

BIKES

FREE PLAY

BASKET-BALL

INTERMEDIATE FIELD GAMES

& RAILROAD TRACKS

CORN FIELD

LITTLE-LEAGUE BASEBALL

FOOTBALL

LEGEND

⇒⇒ AUTO-TRUCK TRAFFIC

⇒⇒ BICYCLE PATH

▭▭▭ MAJOR PEDESTRIAN WAY

▫▫▫▫ MINOR PEDESTRIAN WAY

········· EXISTING CONTOURS

——— PROPOSED CONTOURS

PROGRAMMED FIELD GAMES

NORTH

FUTURE RESIDENCES

LINE OF PARK-SCHOOL PROPERTY DIVISION

0   50   100   200

NOTE:
CONTOUR INTERVAL
EQUALS TWO FEET

7·3

A SCHOOL PARK SITE PLAN · SOLUTION 1

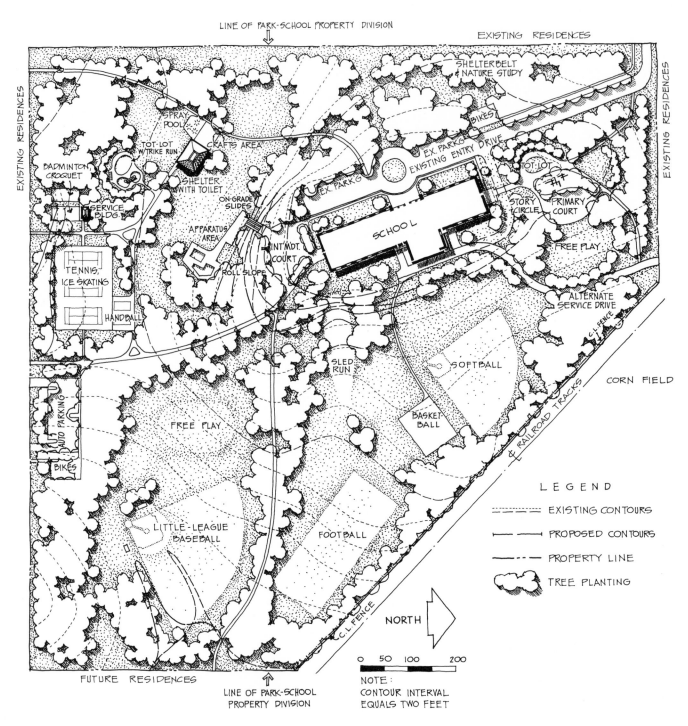

LINE OF PARK-SCHOOL PROPERTY DIVISION

EXISTING RESIDENCES

SHELTERBELT & NATURE STUDY

EXISTING RESIDENCES

EXISTING RESIDENCES

BIKES

SPRAY POOL

CRAFTS AREA

EX. PARK'G
EXISTING ENTRY DRIVE

TOT-LOT

TOT-LOT W/TRIKE RUN

EX. PARK'G

STORY CIRCLE

PRIMARY COURT

BADMINTON CROQUET

SHELTER WITH TOILET

ON-GRADE SLIDES

SCHOOL

FREE PLAY

SERVICE BLDG.

APPARATUS AREA

INT'MDT. COURT

ROLL SLOPE

ALTERNATE SERVICE DRIVE

TENNIS, ICE SKATING

HANDBALL

SLED RUN

SOFTBALL

C.L. FENCE

CORN FIELD

BASKET BALL

RAILROAD TRACKS

AUTO PARKING

FREE PLAY

L E G E N D

BIKES

EXISTING CONTOURS

PROPOSED CONTOURS

LITTLE-LEAGUE BASEBALL

FOOTBALL

PROPERTY LINE

TREE PLANTING

C.L. FENCE

NORTH

FUTURE RESIDENCES

LINE OF PARK-SCHOOL PROPERTY DIVISION

0 50 100   200

NOTE:
CONTOUR INTERVAL
EQUALS TWO FEET

7·4

A SCHOOL PARK   SITE PLAN - SOLUTION 2

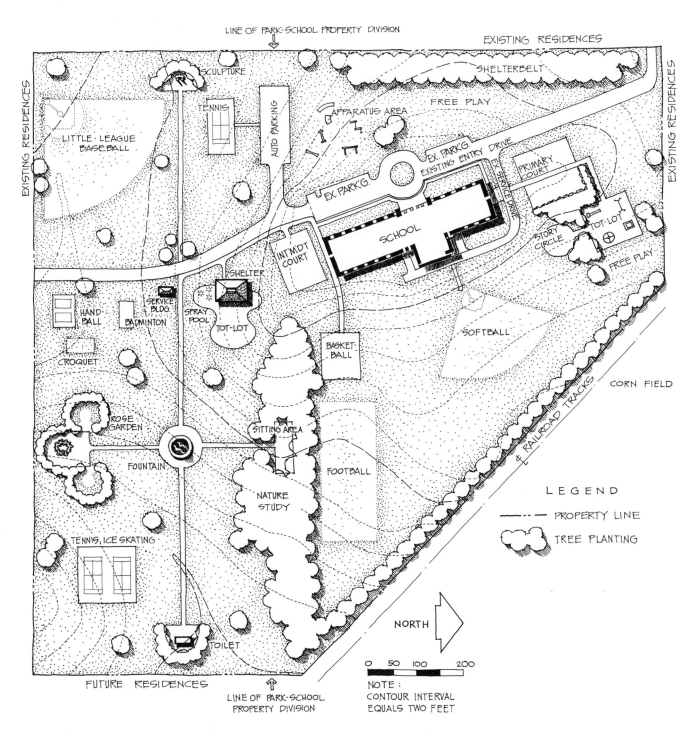

LINE OF PARK-SCHOOL PROPERTY DIVISION

EXISTING RESIDENCES

SHELTERBELT

FREE PLAY

SCULPTURE

TENNIS

AUTO PARKING

APPARATUS AREA

EXISTING RESIDENCES

EXISTING RESIDENCES

LITTLE-LEAGUE BASEBALL

EX. PARKG.

EX. PARKG.

EXISTING ENTRY DRIVE

EX. SERVICE DRIVE

PRIMARY COURT

TOT-LOT

SCHOOL

STORY CIRCLE

FREE PLAY

INT'MDT COURT

SHELTER

SERVICE BLDG.

SPRAY POOL

HAND-BALL

BADMINTON

TOT-LOT

BASKET-BALL

SOFTBALL

CROQUET

CORN FIELD

ROSE GARDEN

SITTING AREA

FOUNTAIN

NATURE STUDY

FOOTBALL

RAILROAD TRACKS

LEGEND

PROPERTY LINE

TREE PLANTING

TENNIS, ICE SKATING

NORTH

TOILET

0   50   100   200

FUTURE RESIDENCES

LINE OF PARK-SCHOOL PROPERTY DIVISION

NOTE:
CONTOUR INTERVAL
EQUALS TWO FEET

7·5

A STATE PARK   PROGRAM

UNITS

LODGE BUILDING -
GUEST AND MEETING ROOMS, RESTAURANT, RESERVATION DESK FOR LODGE AND CABINS.

LODGE PARKING -
30 SPACES FOR GUESTS, 50 SPACES FOR GENERAL USE, 10 SPACES FOR EMPLOYEES.

30 HOUSEKEEPING CABINS

CABIN PARKING -
ONE SPACE EACH CONVENIENT TO EACH CABIN.

CAMPING AREA -
200 SITES

FAMILY PICNICKING AREA -
100 SITES

OUTDOOR AMPHITHEATRE

BOAT DOCK -
ROWBOATS, CANOES

WALKING TRAILS

RENTAL STABLE

BRIDLE TRAILS

MAINTENANCE BUILDING AND SERVICE YARD

STAFF HOUSING -
DETACHED HOUSES FOR MANAGER AND ASSISTANT MANAGER AND FAMILIES.

CRITERION

PROVIDE OPPORTUNITIES TO EXPERIENCE THE NATURAL QUALITIES OF THE SITE.

7·6

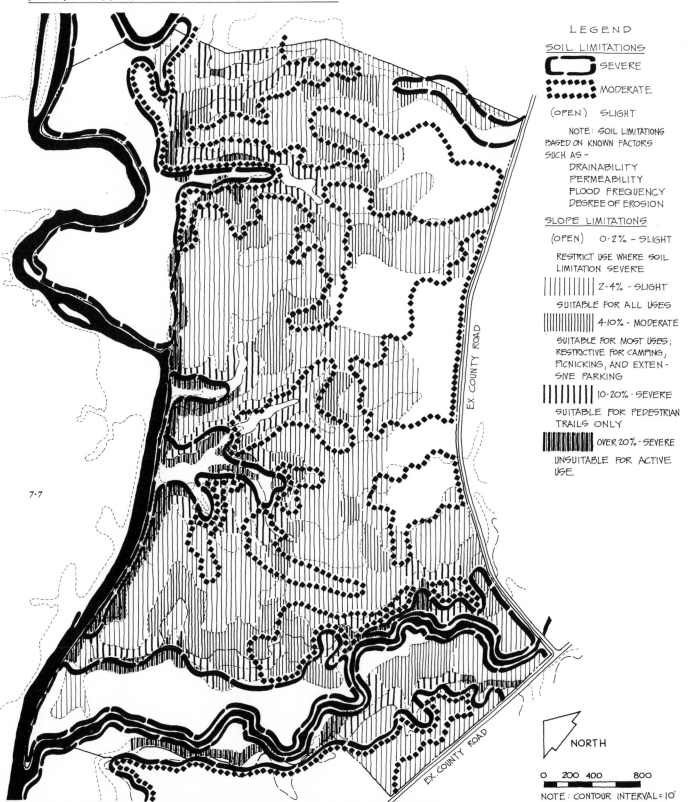

LEGEND

SOIL LIMITATIONS

SEVERE

MODERATE

(OPEN) SLIGHT

NOTE: SOIL LIMITATIONS
BASED ON KNOWN FACTORS
SUCH AS -
DRAINABILITY
PERMEABILITY
FLOOD FREQUENCY
DEGREE OF EROSION

SLOPE LIMITATIONS

(OPEN) 0-2% - SLIGHT

RESTRICT USE WHERE SOIL
LIMITATION SEVERE

2-4% - SLIGHT

SUITABLE FOR ALL USES

4-10% - MODERATE

SUITABLE FOR MOST USES;
RESTRICTIVE FOR CAMPING,
PICNICKING, AND EXTEN-
SIVE PARKING

10-20% - SEVERE

SUITABLE FOR PEDESTRIAN
TRAILS ONLY

OVER 20% - SEVERE

UNSUITABLE FOR ACTIVE
USE

7·7

EX. COUNTY ROAD

EX. COUNTY ROAD

NORTH

0   200 400   800

NOTE: CONTOUR INTERVAL = 10'

A STATE PARK

SITE ANALYSIS 2 OF 2

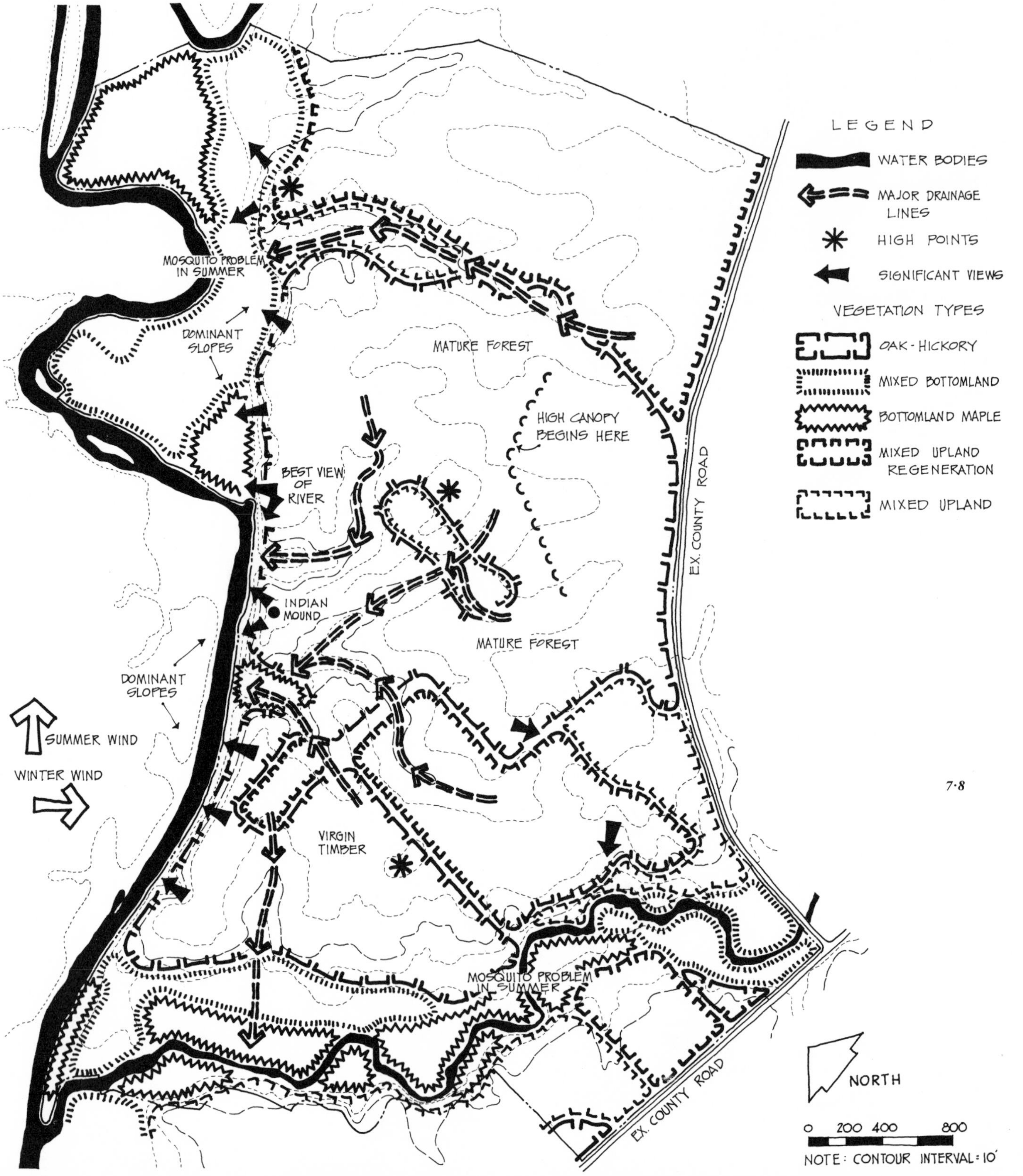

LEGEND
WATER BODIES
MAJOR DRAINAGE LINES
HIGH POINTS
SIGNIFICANT VIEWS
VEGETATION TYPES
OAK-HICKORY
MIXED BOTTOMLAND
BOTTOMLAND MAPLE
MIXED UPLAND REGENERATION
MIXED UPLAND
MOSQUITO PROBLEM IN SUMMER
DOMINANT SLOPES
MATURE FOREST
HIGH CANOPY BEGINS HERE
BEST VIEW OF RIVER
INDIAN MOUND
MATURE FOREST
DOMINANT SLOPES
SUMMER WIND
WINTER WIND
VIRGIN TIMBER
MOSQUITO PROBLEM IN SUMMER
EX. COUNTY ROAD
EX. COUNTY ROAD
NORTH
0 200 400 800
NOTE: CONTOUR INTERVAL = 10'

7·8

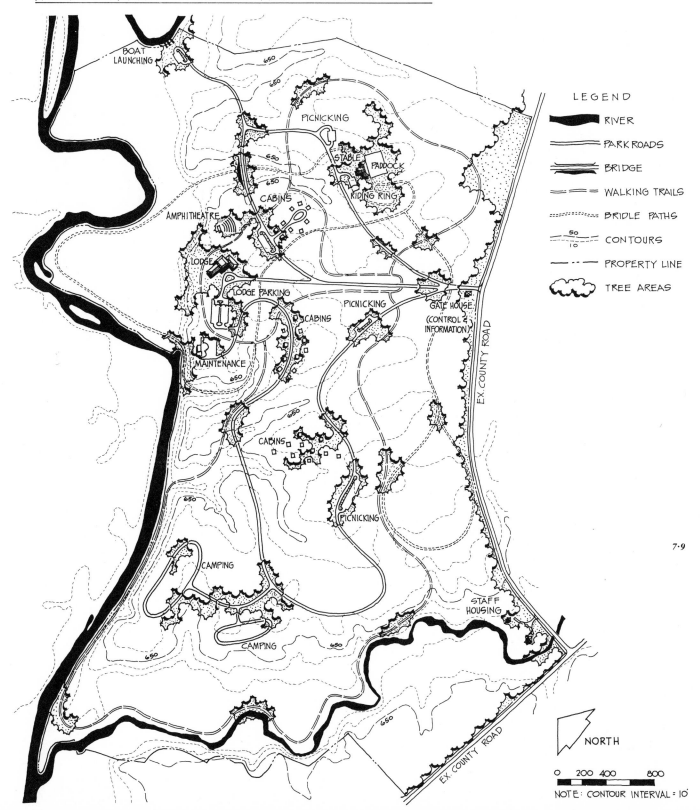

A STATE PARK   MASTER PLAN - SOLUTION 1

BOAT LAUNCHING

PICNICKING

STABLE   PADDOCK

RIDING RING

CABINS

AMPHITHEATRE

LODGE

LODGE PARKING

PICNICKING

GATE HOUSE
(CONTROL &
INFORMATION)

CABINS

MAINTENANCE

EX. COUNTY ROAD

CABINS

PICNICKING

CAMPING

STAFF
HOUSING

CAMPING

7·9

LEGEND

RIVER

PARK ROADS

BRIDGE

WALKING TRAILS

BRIDLE PATHS

50
10   CONTOURS

PROPERTY LINE

TREE AREAS

EX. COUNTY ROAD

NORTH

0   200 400   800

NOTE: CONTOUR INTERVAL = 10'

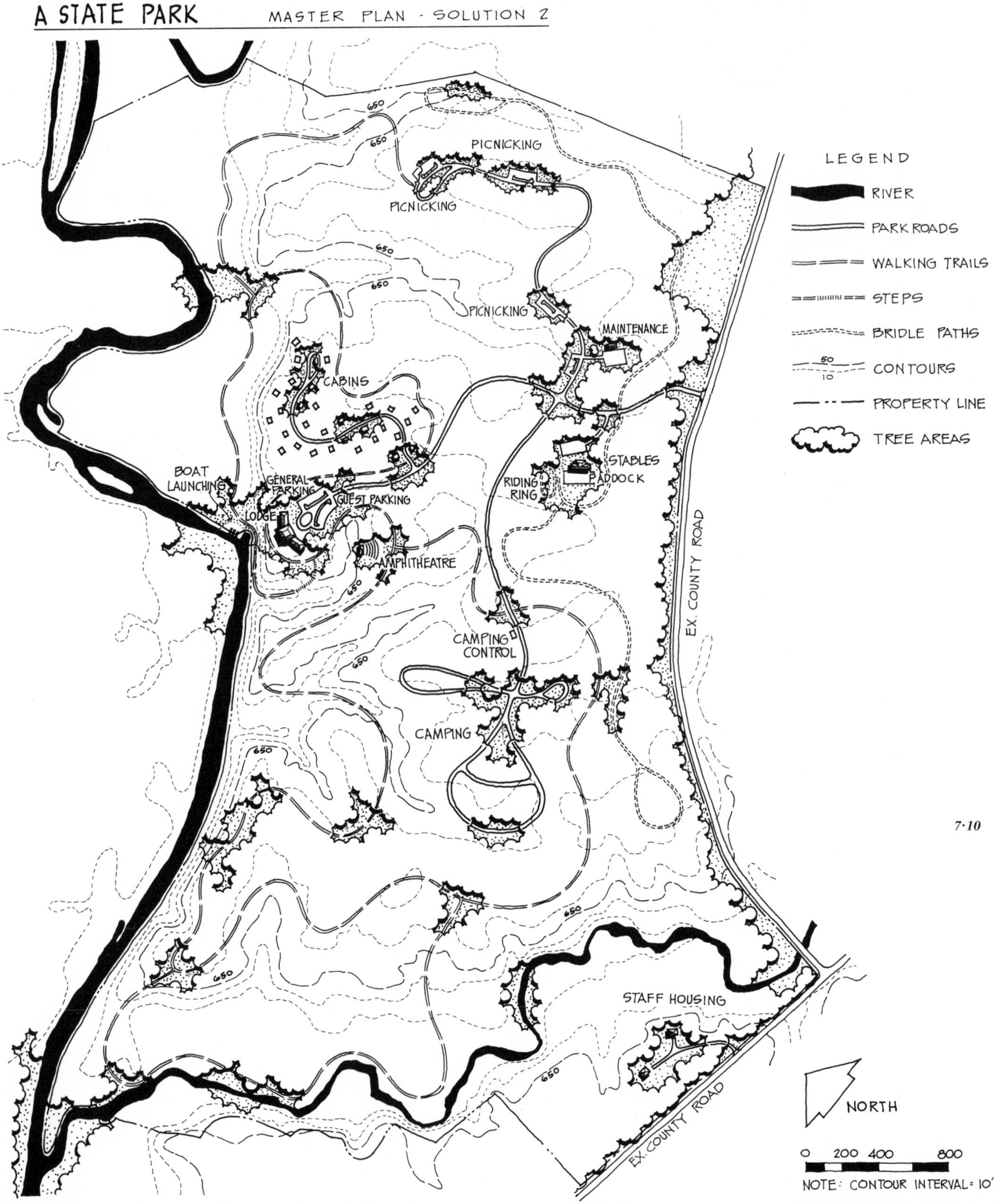

A STATE PARK   MASTER PLAN · SOLUTION 2

PICNICKING

PICNICKING

PICNICKING

PICNICKING

MAINTENANCE

CABINS

STABLES
PADDOCK

RIDING
RING

BOAT
LAUNCHING

GENERAL
PARKING

GUEST PARKING

LODGE

AMPHITHEATRE

CAMPING
CONTROL

CAMPING

STAFF HOUSING

EX. COUNTY ROAD

EX. COUNTY ROAD

LEGEND

	RIVER
	PARK ROADS
	WALKING TRAILS
	STEPS
	BRIDLE PATHS
50 / 10	CONTOURS
	PROPERTY LINE
	TREE AREAS

7·10

NORTH

0   200 400   800

NOTE: CONTOUR INTERVAL = 10'

AN URBAN PARKLET   PROGRAM

UNITS _____   CRITERIA

   1) BENCHES
   2) DRINKING FOUNTAIN
   3) WASTE CANS
   4) APPROPRIATE PLANTING
   5) WALKWAYS

   1) ACCOMMODATE PEDESTRIAN
      MOVEMENT PATTERNS.
   2) PROVIDE SITTING AREAS FOR
      SHOPPERS AND BUS PATRONS.

7·11

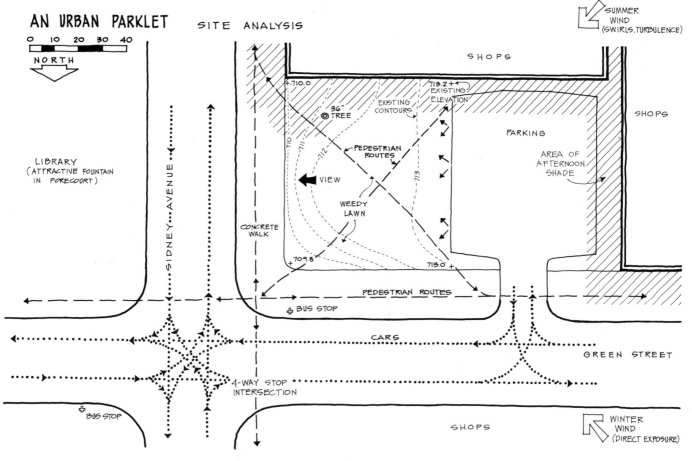

7·12

AN URBAN PARKLET

SITE PLAN SOLUTION 1

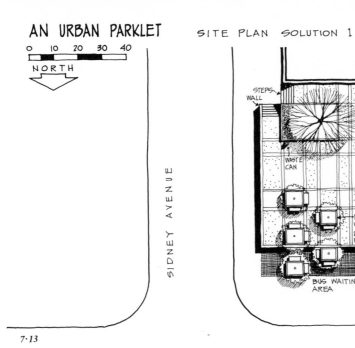
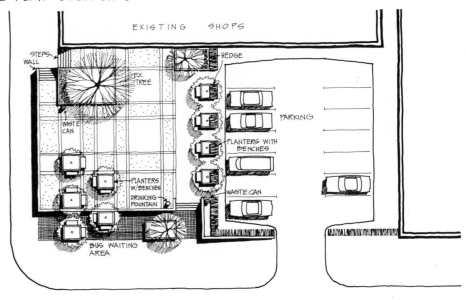

0 10 20 30 40

NORTH

EXISTING SHOPS

STEPS
WALL
EX. TREE
WASTE CAN
PLANTERS W/BENCHES
DRINKING FOUNTAIN
BUS WAITING AREA

HEDGE
PARKING
PLANTERS WITH BENCHES
WASTE CAN

SIDNEY AVENUE

GREEN STREET

7·13

AN URBAN PARKLET

SITE PLAN SOLUTION 2

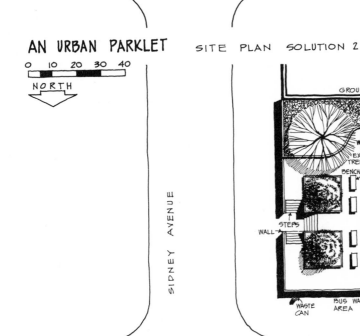
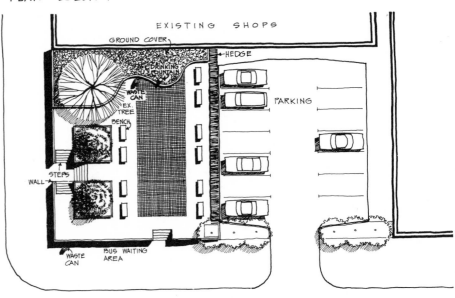

0 10 20 30 40

NORTH

EXISTING SHOPS

GROUND COVER
HEDGE
DRINKING FOUNTAIN
WASTE CAN
EX. TREE
BENCH
WALL
STEPS
WASTE CAN
BUS WAITING AREA

PARKING

SIDNEY AVENUE

GREEN STREET

7·14

Both problems and solutions are presented in simplified form in deference to the assumption that these are among your first attempts to evaluate a design proposal. You should also be aware of the fact that a complete examination of program and site requires more knowledge of prevailing circumstances than can be read from the provided program and map. For instance, acceding to the demands of brevity and other limitations of the printed page, little is indicated regarding surrounding influences and nothing describes applicable ordinances. Unavailable too are the nuances known to someone who has walked the site and is familiar with the locality and the affected population. While this knowledge would be handy in actual circumstances, enough complexity and information is presented in these hypothetical cases to confront you with a meaningful challenge.

In evaluating these cases, until you become quite acquainted with professionally prepared plans and their ingredients, it is suggested that you attempt to follow the procedure outlined in this chapter from preparation to critique. This is not to promote the procedure as the only one possible, nor is it to imply that everyone will feel comfortable in its use. Indeed, there are circumstances where it will prove to be unwieldy, but since it is comprehensive and offers a technique for unearthing specific determinants, its use at the onset should encourage the development of similar traits in whatever other system is eventually embraced. During neophyte periods, its steps should give order and fullness to the review, subsequently serving as a plane of departure from which a personal pattern of striking at the anatomy of a park plan may be developed. Such a pattern is sure to emerge as maneuvers become progressively automatic.

Evaluation: A School-park Site Plan.
Solution #1 (Figs. 7.1 through 7.4)

Note: The solution which is the subject of this evaluation was adapted from a plan for the Thomas Paine School-Park, Urbana, Illinois, prepared for the Urbana School District and the Urbana Park District by Phillip E. DeTurk, Landscape Architect.

Goal Validity

1. The need to separate school units from park areas seems appropriate. To minimize the chaos which could be caused by

competition for facilities, an organizational system must be developed which will allow vacationing adults, tots and mothers, housewives on afternoon breaks, and others who might be in the park during school hours to have free run of the areas of highest attraction to them. Yet, their noise and physical presence must be kept out of the hair of school kids and teachers. Separation should pose no difficulty. The trick will be to satisfy the seemingly contradictory demand—the fusing of school and park facilities so that after-hours and summer programs can be efficiently administered over the entire site.

A qualification is in order. Essential to the success of any school-park operation is a prearranged agreement between school and park authorities regarding responsibility for the staffing, maintenance, and assumption of injury liability when one authority's program is in effect upon another agency's land. Unless this is spelled out and followed through, the concept is in trouble no matter how well the facilities are organized.

2. Arguing against the provision of educational experiences is like disparaging motherhood and apple pie, especially in a development associated with a school.

3. Foresight would have eliminated the need to establish the financially wasteful third criterion. For while traffic on the service road is only sporadic, hence posing but a moderate hazard, the fact that the road exists at all in its present location illustrates in microcosm what can happen when coordination in the design of the building and site is missing.

The school structure was sited and built before the landscape architect was approached to consider the rest of the land. When the landscape architect is not present to consult with the building architect, a view toward the entire development is missing. As a result, the building architect, unable to judge the effects of his acts upon land-use efficiency, may very well divide up land suited for companion use units by access roads, locate buildings on land more appropriate for other purposes, etc. This also works in reverse. When laboring in isolation, the landscape architect may tie down a building to a place on the site which could pose restrictions to the design of the structure. What should have been called for, as it should be in any project comprising buildings and extensive land usage, was a collaborative study of the entire 33 acres by building architect and landscape architect treating the full acreage as a single problem.

However, hindsight will not rectify this issue. Since the service road abuts the building at the door out of which the kindergarten kids are expected to flood, and it can be anticipated that those in this age group will be oblivious to the potential danger, the road should be relocated. Although traffic is sporadic, the prospect of but one accident chills the alternative of leaving it alone.

4. Those who have experienced central Illinois know it as a flat sheet of corn and soybean fields served up in proportions guaranteed to anaesthetize the senses. Too much of a muchness, as one wag has put it. The need to secure environmental diversity is therefore a worthy criterion. The manner in which it is provided deserves special attention because, even though its basic charge is to instill variety, the plan must also ensure the retention of the character of the place in order to avoid the embarrassment of establishing a 33-acre sore thumb.

The Complex-at-large

Goal Realization   Separation is brought about simply by placing most of the school units on school property and the majority of park facilities on the park-owned land. No big deal. However, design expertise receives a standing ovation for the balancing act it causes the use areas within each property to perform. Note first of all that the tennis and handball courts and the totlot and park shelter, which are units of high attraction for school-hour park visitors, are placed at some distance from the school building, which also puts them handy to the park entrance. Thereby, the park population is concentrated where conflict is unlikely to occur during school hours. In addition, the park's apparatus and free play space, which may have minor use during the school day, but be major attractions after classes let out, are separated from the building by sloping topography. But, at the same time, they are made to flow from the school's intermediate court to be available if school leaders desire. Now, refocus on this quadrant. And you can see a complete activity setup suited to an after-hours or summer program for young children, with the shelter serving as a centrally located supervisory station.

By virtue of its proximity to both the school's intermediate court and game fields, the free play area can be used in conjunction with the former and as overflow for the latter, thus creating use possibilities for the park's open area which might otherwise lie fallow during school hours. Flowing together, yet gingerly separated, the full complement of school-park fields offers a range of combinations for evening, weekend, or summer sport programs—big areas, small areas, places for structured events such as playground tournaments, spaces for unprogrammed activities such as kite flying, model airplane soaring, or just plain running around. Between scheduled events, the field half of the site is an ideal arena for satisfying whim—from pick-up games to unpredictable role playing, up and down its slopes, under and around its trees, in its small and large spaces—for it is well buffered from the game courts and the youngest children's activity areas where greater use control must be exercised.

A break in this pattern may be noted; the basketball court is located near the softball field rather than proximate to the tennis courts where it would be more available for adult school-hour use. However, since it has been requested as a school-related unit and is likely to be of greatest attraction to the after-school set, its location removed from the other courts seems justified.

Therefore, the layout appears to meet the first goal; it contains enough flexibility to fit a range of use combinations, yet has an appropriate number of relationship safeguards to ward off use conflicts. There is only one major duplication, that being the totlots which show up both north and south. This appears unavoidable since totlots may be demanded by both residents and kindergarteners during the same hours. In addition, it is as reasonable to place the school's lot next to related classrooms as it is to site the other near the park entrance. With the building already in place, there is no way a single area can meet these requirements. But even here, the designer is on his creative toes, providing the park's lot with a trike run thereby lending it a special facility and flavor. Coincidently, a bonus is gained by the provision of two tot areas. After school hours and during the weekends and summer, residents to the north have a lot more convenient to their homes than the one slated for the park proper.

To the possibilities for education which already exist on the site—the proximity of the railroad, including the original prairie grasses which still grow along its right-of-way, the adjacency of the cornfields reflecting the region's agricultural heritage—the designer has added a nature study shelterbelt and encouraged human interaction by providing several congregating catalysts. Judgments regarding other measures such as the suitability of the crafts facility and the educational horizons of the play apparatus must wait until more detail can be seen, inasmuch as, for these, the scale prohibits full disclosure of the designer's intentions.

The suggestion of the nature study area illustrates the turning of a liability into an advantage. Shortly before the preparation of this plan, the roof of the school was lifted from its rafters by storm winds, scattering its pieces to Munchkin Land. Fortunately, children were not in the building at the time. Wind screening is therefore advisable, lest it happen again with more dire results. To the designer, the shelterbelt translates into a nature study place, thereby exploiting the dual-use principle. Happily, the space into which the grove was directed, the designer having no choice as to its location, lies adjacent to the school and reaches conveniently toward the park shelter from which interpretive programs can emanate.

While human interaction can go on wherever there are people, in this plan design ploys have intensified the possibility. The park shelter, centrally placed to generate observation of child play, and the spectator slopes, located convenient to the softball and little league fields, are two which are immediately evident. Other potentials as sitting spaces associated with totlots and game courts remain to be exploited in further detail studies.

The turning of an obstacle into an asset also distinguishes the handling of the service-drive relocation. Once obstructing the passage from the classrooms to the area best suited for primary play, the road now separates younger activity from the older kids' sport fields, thereby discouraging overlap where a need to do so exists. The drive still nestles next to the gym, but this seems unavoidable due to the previously set location of the building's service docks. While such a pavement expanse at the foot of the building will still look like hell, the remaining safety problem is relatively negligible. It can be assumed that traffic movement has subsided at this point, the road becoming primarily a storage and maneuvering surface, and that the older children passing across the pavement will be more alert to the presence of vehicles than the primary graders.

Toward instilling environmental variety, the designer is in luck, for the site sits on one of the glacial moraines which occasionally interrupt the pervasive horizontality of the region. As fortunate as he might have been to begin with, the manner in which the landscape architect has followed through must be logged to his personal credit. Recognizing that the site itself is a welcome contrast to the surrounding rule, the designer has intensified what exists, thereby managing order and variety with the same stroke. Use units have been settled into existing pockets formed by the site's rolling topography. The sculptural character of the ridges has been accented with brows of tree masses. And to ensure that users experience the views associated with the changes of grade, collector walkways have been placed on the crests of the topographical rolls.

Relation of Park to Surroundings The shelterbelt screens the school's parking lot and entry road from residences to the west. Reaches of pavement required by tennis and parking to the south are also adequately buffered from residential view. The totlots are guarded from surrounding traffic by distance and plantings. Highly concentrated use has been kept away from the railroad. The chain-link fence proposed to edge the right-of-way should keep bouncing balls from the tracks, whereas the high trees should handle errant flies. The fence should also thwart wandering on to the roadbed when teacher supervision is not present.

Relation of Use Areas to Site In addition to recognizing the existence of topographic pockets, the designer has correctly regarded variations in grade as a distinguishing characteristic of the site. In matching uses to the land, he has been faithful to the following realities regarding relative slope severity:

1. Since slopes of 0 to 2 percent are essentially flat and the soil which covers the entire site heavy and resistant to immediate percolation, drainage would be slow if planted in lawn, but rapid if paved. Hence, slopes of this type are suited for court games: basketball, tennis, vollyball, dodgeball, etc.

2. Slopes in the 2 to 4 percent range are fairly flat, yet steep enough to provide adequate surface water runoff if planted in lawn. These slopes are appropriate for sport fields: softball, baseball, football, soccer, etc.

3. Slopes ranging from 4 to 10 percent have rapid surface runoff, but are too steep for organized field sports or court games. If planted in lawn and intensive use imposed, erosion

could be a major problem. Slopes of this type can be used for general free play where use is sporadic and does not conform to a set pattern.

4. Slopes over 10 percent are too severe for concentrated use. Erosion is a definite problem requiring such slopes to be stabilized with ground covers, rough-cut lawns, trees, etc. These grades should receive only intermittent traffic or special use where steep pitches are essential to the play experience (see built-in slides, sled run, roll slope, etc., on the plan). They can also serve to separate incompatible activities.

Only slight earth reshaping is suggested to accommodate the appropriate matches. This occurs notably south of the school, extending the existing shelf to a size adequate for intermediate court installation, and near the tennis courts to the southwest and the little league field to the southeast. The latter moves relocate the existing swales in order to improve drainability, yet allow the site's natural drainage pattern to remain intact.

Relation of Use Areas to Use Areas   Most of these dealings have been covered under goal realization. In addition, it is noted that the park's automobile lot is located central to the game courts and little league field, which makes sense inasmuch as these facilities will draw many adults who might be inclined to arrive by auto. Primary adult attractions—tennis, handball, badminton, etc.—are well buffered from nearby play areas slated for youngsters.

Relation of Major Structures to Use Areas   While students deserve a better view from the western windows than that which is provided by the parking lot, the landscape architect had no control over the location of the lot and entry drive; their placement was determined when the building was constructed. Since the kindergarten to second grades occupy the north wing of the school, the immediacy of the totlot and primary court is advisable. There is similar wisdom in the proposed location for the intermediate court, inasmuch as it rests adjacent to the door which leads to the third to sixth grades. Commotion associated with these areas is subdued somewhat by plantings. The playfields are handy to the gym entrance, noise being minimized by distance.

Circulation   As has been stated, vehicular access and parking lots for the school were set before the site study was begun, and the relocation of the service drive has already been discussed. In addition, the parking lot to the south sits on the park periphery, happily minimizing vehicular penetration of the grounds.

Bicycle routes also penetrate the site only slightly, thereby freeing the bulk of the acreage for unimpeded pedestrian travel. It is proposed that bicycles be stored both near the school and on the park in spaces approximate to the auto parking lots, which seems reasonable, although after alighting bicyclists must cross the entry drive to get to the school entrance, presumably at the same time that school officials are driving up the road to the building. This bug remains to be worked out of the scheme. Separate bicycle lanes are wisely suggested to avoid the hazards of mixing pedestrians with wheeled vehicles.

Pedestrian access seems sufficient with walking routes across the park providing for a direct flow to the school. This is certainly necessary due to the amount of daily traffic seeking that objective. The fact that walks follow the ridgelines wherever possible not only suggests the availability of views, but ensures quick drainage during inclement weather as well. Paved access from the gym to the basketball courts and ballfields also eases the need for follow-up maintenance when the ground is soggy.

The three-prong circuit from the southern and eastern edges to the school additionally serves as collector routes for the park from which secondary walkways extend to various interior facilities. Walks are adroitly placed between use units so as not to interfere with play, for the most part also acting as psychological barriers between separate facilities.

Field areas need no more access than has been provided inasmuch as entry patterns are unpredictable and stepping-off spaces varied. Since service circulation for park maintenance would be minimal, the walkway system or lawn areas could be used as necessary.

Spatial Experiences   A full assessment of spatial character requires a review of commitments still to be arrived at during subsequent detail studies. However, at the scale being dealt with here, it is essential that the designer set up the overall three-dimensional network to which he will relate his follow-up thinking. Therefore, what deserves attention on this plan is evidence of a spatial structure per se. This landscape architect has met the objective well, compartmentalizing use units with tree masses or in topographic pockets which he has reinforced with plant material, closing off one compartment from another where separation is advisable, and linking others where circulation or viewing suggests a need to do so.

A clue to a designer's sensitivity for three-dimensional thinking is found in his massing of major plant material in contrast to the alternative of scattering isolated trees about as if they were thrown at a dart board by a drunken marksman. Where the former is in evidence on a large-scale plan, there is an excellent chance that detail studies will lead to substantial and appropriate spatial qualities. However, if space is not considered at the larger scales, as exemplified by an inebriated attitude toward the plantings, it is unlikely that it will seep into further handling of the project.

Aesthetic Character Total evaluation of the proposal's aesthetic qualities must also wait until the design of each use unit can be seen in full detail. However, as with spatial structure, what can be sensed from this scale is *potential* for substance and appropriateness as indicated by the general lie of lines, forms, textures, colors, and spaces. While not final commitments, these record what the designer has in mind and will strive to develop when pursuing later studies.

The lines, forms, and spatial network should be given the closest attention. At the scale this plan has been drawn, textures and colors are used primarily to separate out the various ground surfaces to enhance the drawing's appeal and readability. However, at the same time, they might also reflect something about the project's relative liveliness or sterility.

Are there experiences provided? Will they be substantial? This plan seems to say yes, for it contains not only a strong spatial structure but a consistent form flavor as well. *Both* spatial and line configurations move about the site in spirited fashion, complementing each other and hinting that the designer has indeed opted toward a dominant effect.

Will the effect be appropriate? The answer once more appears to be yes, for the plan's parts have been endowed with an animated and playful feeling, well in keeping with the purpose of a recreational enterprise of this type. The organic quality about the spaces and forms also suggests a fidelity to the rolling sense of the site.

Order and Variety   Points already discussed, such as fitting use units into topographic hollows, remaining faithful to slope aspects, intensifying existing site character, etc., leave little doubt that the blending of new with old will come off successfully, thereby fostering environmental order.

Variety potential shows up in the tree-accented topographic changes, varying sizes and configurations of spatial openings, and the exploitation of view possibilities. Additional enrichment should arise from the detailing of the use areas and selection of plant species. While these remain to be accomplished, the fact that the designer has indicated such a degree of feeling for the matter within the restrictions posed by the plan scale gives a reasonable assurance that his detail augmentation will be equally successful. A less confident posture would have to be struck were the designer lax in presenting such clues to his aesthetic sensitivity.

Each Use Area in Turn

Some general comments are in order before proceeding on the tour of the use units. Since additional design steps are required after acceptance of this plan, focus upon each area may trigger suggestions to be incorporated into ensuing detail studies. It benefits both client and designer to think ahead in order to initiate further study on a basis of mutual agreement. Thoughts augmenting those shown on the plan are usually volunteered by the designer or brought out by the client with the asking of the question: "What else do you have in mind for this area?" Therefore, as might occur during the course of a typical design presentation, ideas for future study are expressed in the following. The reader must clearly distinguish these from objections which are also raised.

Turning back to the plan in general, the first thing which is noticed is that use units not originally required by the program are proposed. The additions all seem compatible with project purposes and fit their places among the other areas. The service building and facilities for handball, badminton, croquet, tricycling, and bike parking are adjuncts to initially specified units. The nature-study shelterbelt and sled run are further exploitations of the site. Assuming that the designer has determined that such activities are expressive of a neighborhood need, plaudits are due for appropriately broadening the use of the property.

In addition, it is noted that all areas seem to be sized properly and oriented correctly. An exception in the latter category is the sled run slated for an eastern slope. Such a compromise with ideal orientation may be excused, for the run is located where the greatest length of steep surface is found on the site.

By now, evaluation has been almost completed, for during the complex-at-large investigation, much has been said about the functional and aesthetic reasonableness of each use unit. This round will begin with the school's totlot, then move clockwise, stopping at each area to clean up what might have been missed previously.

Interior circulation works well north of the building, for the route to the primary court bypasses the totlot, thereby minimizing interruptions. By its location, the free-play turf can nicely handle overflow from the court. The entire cluster can be readily supervised from one spot. Also easing supervision, the totlot is well contained by plantings as is the free-play space, the latter safely barricaded from the service road. In his detail studies, it is hoped that the designer will retain the flowing forms and provide rich material contrasts in order to stimulate imaginations and sensory faculties. It is also hoped that equipment design will provide for a full range of play experiences — sliding, climbing, running, jumping, rolling, balancing, and digging. In this rather small space, this will probably mean the inclusion of several multipurpose pieces, inasmuch as the square footage does not appear adequate for many separate items.

The basketball court will have to be buffered from the softball diamond foul line. Visual supervision of the entire field sports area can take place from the walkway. In the actual placement of trees on the sledding slope, the need to maintain unobstructed sliding channels must be considered. Utilizing the vacant ballfields for the sled landing exemplifies exploitation of the dual-use principle.

Affording a view of the little league field, the nearby mound should attract spectators, thereby encouraging the experiencing of the highest point in the park. The adjacent free-play space can be used for practice and little league tryouts, establishing another possibility for dual usage.

Dual use also shows up in the designer's thinking in the employment of the tennis courts for ice skating. Surfacing material which can withstand the rigors of freezing or thawing yet remain suitable for tennis will have to be selected to make this work. Expansion possibilities for the tennis courts seems to be thwarted due to their being hemmed in on all sides by other construction. Tennis demand is frequently underestimated, and if the clamor for more courts should rear up, a real problem exists. To make the courts available for those whose working schedule permits only evening play, night lighting should be considered in the detail thinking as should sitting accommodations for those crowded days when players must wait their turns. By being centrally located among the tennis, badminton, and croquet areas, the service house can be used to control reservations and equipment loans.

The tricycle circuit suggested for the totlot can lead to a host of fun possibilities if eventually laid out with varying curves, grade changes, tunnels, etc. Some design precautions will have to be taken to minimize conflict with whatever more-sedentary pursuits are planned for in the same area. As with the north lot, seating accommodations should be slated for the comfort of supervising parents.

The play spaces surrounding the park shelter are clustered well, allowing sweeping visual inspection from the shelter at the hub of the complex. The spray pool (a safety problem) and crafts area (requiring direct student-teacher contact) are wisely made to abut the shelter. However, measures will have to be taken to keep wind whipped spray in check. Further exploiting dual-use possibilities, the crafts surface and structure may serve for small group picnics held as part of a summer playground program. This leads to the thought that the shelter might contain equipment storage facilities and an outdoor fireplace, but raises a question about the inclusion of toilets. While a convenient comfort station is desirable, the flushing sounds sure to escape through the walls might very well dull appetites. Perhaps public toilets could be incorporated into the service building a few yards south, thereby providing a handy convenience for adults as well.

Situated well on the other side of the shelter from the totlot in order to minimize age-group conflict, the on-grade slides, apparatus, and roll slope combination present intriguing possibilities for stimulating play. The plan sets this up as an action area which should be carried through in the detailing. Accordingly, criteria for selecting apparatus should include the pieces' potential for stimulating adventures, fostering role playing, and triggering imaginations. Grass chosen for adjacent slopes should be the toughest strains in anticipation of the activity which is encouraged upon them.

To fully exploit the potential of the shelterbelt as a nature area, possibilities should be included for not only plant identification but insect, bird, and small wildlife study as well. The grove should therefore be allowed to mature in its own ecological way, with undergrowth taking over as a matter of natural course. This rules out grass mowing. Undoubtedly, to get the shelterbelt going, the installation of small trees will be called for, since it would be financially prohibitive immediately to cover such an expanse with mature specimens. Accordingly, if the plan is to be implemented in phases, the belt should be included in the first stage. Then it can be growing to full usefulness while funds for the remaining work are being pursued.

Objects within Each Use Area

Other than that which has been put forward speculating upon the future, no questions can be directed to this plan regarding such individual items as drinking fountains, curbs, drainage catch basins, trash receptacles, etc. Critical commentary upon the propriety of objects within each use area must wait until commitments at detail scale are seen.

Summary

Distinguished by balanced attention to aesthetics and function, order and variety, spatial and ground patterns, use freedom and control, people and mechanical devices—and an organizational system tailored to the site which separates school from park yet produces an overlap appropriately patterned for maximum use flexibility—this is an excellent plan. Most questions of concern involve matters easily handled in the detail stage without affecting the major components of the proposal. The only real problem foreseen is the difficulty of expanding the tennis courts. If they are on top of demand, park authorities can readily judge the degree of risk involved. Hence, the decision to revise the court area or leave it as proposed rests in their hands.

Etcetera

*I*n any geographical area, it is unlikely that all the people's recreation needs can be met on one site in one park. It is more usual that a number of parks are required. This collection of sites to serve the collective need is the "park system" whose planning involves the following steps:

1. It begins with an inventory of existing park lands, including acreage, location, and activities provided for. This shows where you are.

2. To determine where you might go, existing acreage is compared against national standards considered to be minimum for the population served. For instance, such standards suggest that a small city or town should have 10 acres of park land for every 1,000 people. Thus, a raw goal is established.

3. The next step is to determine where the land with the greatest recreation potential is situated within the district. This is

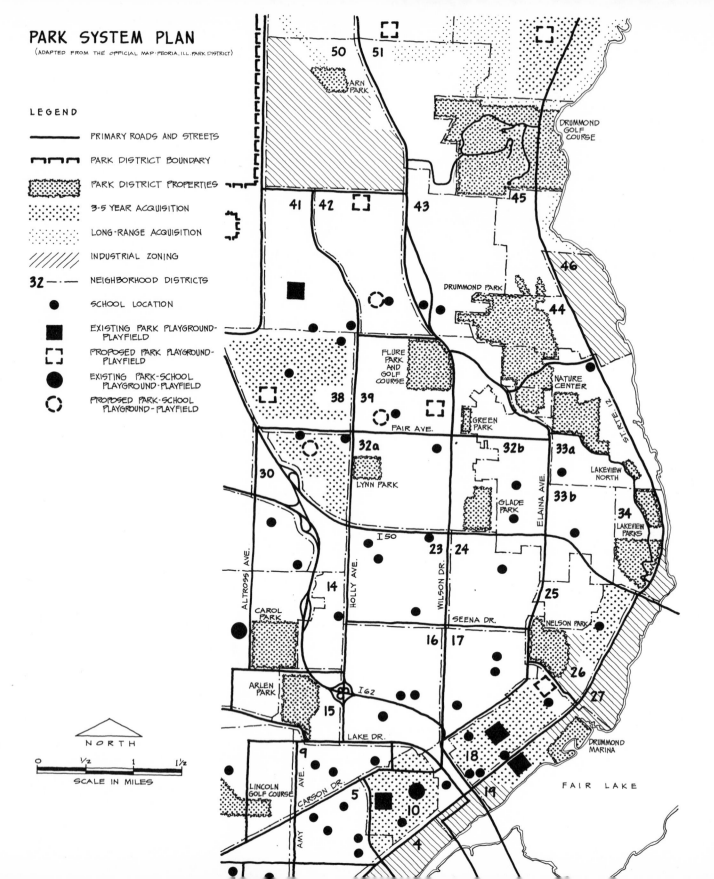

PARK SYSTEM PLAN

(ADAPTED FROM THE OFFICIAL MAP·PEORIA,ILL·PARK DISTRICT)

LEGEND

PRIMARY ROADS AND STREETS

PARK DISTRICT BOUNDARY

PARK DISTRICT PROPERTIES

3·5 YEAR ACQUISITION

LONG-RANGE ACQUISITION

INDUSTRIAL ZONING

32 — NEIGHBORHOOD DISTRICTS

● SCHOOL LOCATION

■ EXISTING PARK PLAYGROUND-PLAYFIELD

PROPOSED PARK PLAYGROUND-PLAYFIELD

● EXISTING PARK-SCHOOL PLAYGROUND-PLAYFIELD

PROPOSED PARK-SCHOOL PLAYGROUND-PLAYFIELD

NORTH

0   ½   1   1½

SCALE IN MILES

ARN PARK

DRUMMOND GOLF COURSE

50   51

41   42   43   45

46

DRUMMOND PARK   44

FLURE PARK AND GOLF COURSE   NATURE CENTER

38   39   FAIR AVE.   GREEN PARK

32a   32b   33a   LAKEVIEW NORTH

30   LYNN PARK   GLADE PARK   33b   34   LAKEVIEW PARKS

I 50   23   24   25

14   NELSON PARK   26

CAROL PARK   16   17   SEENA DR.   27

ARLEN PARK   I 62   DRUMMOND MARINA

15   LAKE DR.   18   19

9   LINCOLN GOLF COURSE   5   10   4   FAIR LAKE

ALTROSS AVE.   HOLLY AVE.   WILSON DR.   ELAINA AVE.   AMY AVE.   CARSON DR.   STATE 12 identified through analyses of existing natural and cultural conditions. Then studies concerning population concentrations, future growth directions, and leisure-time interests of affected age, sex, ethnic, and income groups are conducted to provide information which will enable one to ascertain what pieces of the high-potential land should actually be acquired.

4. Finally, acquisition priorities are spelled out and avenues of financing are investigated.

The product is the "park system (sometimes called "comprehensive") plan," offered as a map showing the location of both the existing and proposed park sites. Once purchased, each parcel must be given further study to chart its course of development, but many decisions affecting the success of that development have already been made at the stage of acquisition. If the land is not suited to the activities desired, either program or site will have to be compromised. That is, program units will have to be eliminated due to site restrictions, or the site will have to be fouled up in order to shove in nonconforming facilities.

Planning the park system deserves a volume in itself; we cannot even pretend to scratch its surface here. However, well within the context of our dealings with design, out of this brief introduction can come the following recommendations: An expert with a feeling for design and knowledge of development should be a part of the system planning team. Ideally, desired uses should be known before sites are acquired. If this is not possible, *variety* should be a prime criterion ordering the purchase of land. If sites exhibiting a wide range of characteristics are available, there is sure to be a parcel suited to a future need.

When that need arises, design begins. Will it be a quality solution? Remember, you will have to live with the results. So, go on out and have yourself a park.

 *Appendixes*

The following excerpts illustrate the kinds of empirical data and tools available to recreation area designers. You are asked to approach them with the precautions expressed in Chapters 2 and 4 in mind. More extensive tables related to these and other design matters are found in many of the books listed in the bibliography.

APPENDIX 1   Selected Park and Activity Size and Facility Standards

Totlot. 2,400 to 5,000 square feet.

Usually includes: chair swings, sandbox, regular swings, slide, climbing apparatus, wading or spray pool, playhouse, turf area, paved area for wheeled toys, benches.

Neighborhood Playground. 2½ to 10 acres.

Usually includes: play apparatus, turf area, paved court, playfield, story-telling ring, shelter, wading or spray pool, table game area, picnic center.

Neighborhood Park. 2 to 5 acres.

Usually includes: open lawn, trees, shrubbery, walks, benches, focal point such as ornamental pool or fountains, sandbox, play apparatus, table game area.

Community Playfield. 15 to 25 acres.

Usually includes: separate sport fields for men and women, courts for tennis, boccie, horseshoes, shuffleboard, etc., lawn areas for croquet, archery, etc., outdoor swimming pool, band shell, family picnic area, children's playground, running track, day camp center, parking area.

City Park. 100 to 200 acres.

Usually includes: facilities for boating, swimming, picnicking, hiking, field sports, day camp, zoo, arboretum, nature museum.

County Park. 200 acres or more.

Usually includes: preschool play area (3 acres), elementary play area (4 acres), sport fields (15 acres), paved courts (3 acres), multiple-use court (1 acre), family picnic area (30 acres), open area for special events (10 acres), amphitheater (7 acres), natural area (40 acres), parking for 2,000 cars (15 acres), day and weekend camping area (25 acres), clubhouse and recreation center (5 acres), maintenance yard (5 acres), landscaped area (15 acres), service roads (20 acres).

Natural Environment Area. 5-acre minimum—no limit cited.

Usually includes: picnic area (8 acres), tent camping area (6 acres), trailer camping area (6 acres), hiking trails, boat access, boat marina, sight-seeing facilities, parking areas.

Nine-hole Golf Course. 75 acres (double for eighteen holes).

Usually includes: fairways, roughs, greens, and tees (43 acres), clubhouse (.25 acre), parking area and service roads (1.75 acres), natural area (20 acres), landscaped area (10 acres).

Natural Water Body Swimming.

For every 25 linear feet of shoreline: 5,000 square feet for sunbathing, 2,500 square feet for buffer and picnicking, 1,000 square feet of water area for swimming.

Nature Trail. 1 to 2 miles long each.

Fifty people per mile of trail per day.

Rural Hiking Trail.

Forty people per mile of trail per day.

Urban Hiking Trail.

Ninety people per mile of trail per day.

Family Picnic Area within Communities.

Sixteen units per acre, each unit consisting of table and cooking facilities. One off-street car space per unit.

Family Picnic Area outside of Communities. Ninety to one hundred twenty units per area.

Ten to fifteen units per acre, each unit consisting of one table-bench combination with one charcoal-burning stove per two tables; one comfort station per each thirty units serving a

500-foot radius; drinking fountains no further than 150 feet from picnic units; garbage cans in racks near circulation road no further than 150 feet from picnic units, but not near drinking fountain; bulletin board near comfort station.

Campground. Ninety to one hundred twenty units per area.

Four to seven units per acre consisting of one tent area, one table-bench combination, one camp stove, one parking space; one comfort station per each thirty campsites serving a 300-foot radius; drinking fountains, garbage cans, and bulletin board as for picnicking, above.

APPENDIX 2   Recreation Demand Questionnaire

To gather data toward updating the State of Illinois Outdoor Recreation Plan, a document similar to this was distributed to a representative sampling of Illinois residents by the consulting firm Schellie Associates, Inc., a division of Clyde E. Williams & Associates, Indianapolis, Indiana.

ILLINOIS OUTDOOR RECREATION QUESTIONNAIRE

NAME OF YOUR CITY _____

NAME OF YOUR COUNTY _____

Please indicate the number of days (approximately) in 1966 in which you participated in the following activities and check the items which describe your preference. (If you check more than one category, please number in order of actual participation.)

Days
_____Water Sports
_____swimming
_____water skiing
_____motorboating
_____canoeing
_____sailing
_____Walking
_____for pleasure
_____nature walks
_____hiking
_____mountain climbing
_____Fishing
_____Hunting
_____Camping
_____Bicycling
_____Horseback Riding
_____Picnicking

Days
_____Winter Sports
_____skiing
_____ice skating
_____sledding
_____Outdoor Sports
_____golfing
_____archery
_____team sports
_____target shooting
_____baseball
_____tennis
_____Spectator
_____sports
_____outdoor drama, concerts, etc.
_____Auto Driving
_____for pleasure
_____sightseeing

Please list in order of preference your choice of those outdoor recreational activities which are not now available in your area.

1. _____
2. _____
3. _____
4. _____
5. _____
6. _____
7. _____

APPENDIX 3   Leisure Behavior, Attitude, and Opinion Questionnaire

A particularly detailed type of demand questionnaire, a document similar to the following, was distributed to many residents of LaSalle County, Illinois, by the Office of Recreation and Park Resources, University of Illinois at Urbana-Champaign. Data so gathered was used by the Office in preparing the LaSalle County Conservation District Plan.

LASALLE COUNTY STUDY

Please ignore the dark numbers beside the questions. They are for office use only.

1. How many **hours** do you work in an average week? If you do some work at home related to your job, include those hours too. Housewives should figure time spent doing household activities. (Check one)

   1☐ None   4☐ 25 to 34 hours   7☐ 45 to 49 hours
8 2☐ Less than 15   5☐ 35 to 39 hours   8☐ 50 to 59 hours
   3☐ 15 to 24 hours   6☐ 40 to 44 hours   9☐ 60 or more hours

2a. How much vacation time do you **usually** have each year? (Check one)

   1☐ None   4☐ 2 weeks   7☐ Varies
9 2☐ Less than 1 week   5☐ 3 weeks
   3☐ One week   6☐ More than 3 weeks

b. When do you **usually** take your vacation? (Check one)

      1☐ Jan. - Feb.   3☐ May - June   5☐ Sept. - Oct.
10 2☐ Mar. - April   4☐ July - Aug.   6☐ Nov. - Dec.

c. What part of your vacation time **last year** was spent in LaSalle County? (Check one)

      1☐ None   3☐ One-half   5☐ All
11 2☐ One-fourth   4☐ Three-Fourths

d. How do you **most often** spend your vacation? (Check one)

01 ☐ Traveling   05 ☐ Resort areas

02 ☐ Visiting relatives and friends   06 ☐ Camping

12-13 03 ☐ At home   ☐ Other (List)_____

04 ☐ Outdoor water sports

_____

3a. Do you **usually** have weekends free?

1 ☐ No (If no, continue to 4)

14 2 ☐ Yes

b. How do you most often spend your weekend? (Check one)

01 ☐ Traveling

02 ☐ Visiting relatives and friends

15-16 03 ☐ At home

04 ☐ Outdoor water sports

05 ☐ Resort areas

06 ☐ Camping

☐ Other(List)_____

_____

4. What time or times of day, **during the week,** would you most often have free for participation in activities that you would consider recreational? (Check all that apply)

17 ☐ Before 9 a.m.   20 ☐ 3 p.m. − 6 p.m.   22 ☐ After 8 p.m.

18 ☐ 9 a.m. − 12 noon   21 ☐ 7 p.m. − 8 p.m.   23 ☐ None of these

19 ☐ 1 p.m. − 3 p.m.

5. How many **hours** were spent in each of the following activities **yesterday** (week-day) from 6:00 a.m. to 12:00 midnight? (18 hours)

Hours

24-25 a. Work (occupation)   _____

26 b. Sleep   _____

27 c. Work around the house   _____

28 d. Leisure activities   _____

29 e. Personal grooming   _____

30 f. Other   _____

6. How many **hours** were spent in each of the following activities **last Saturday** from 6:00 a.m. to 12:00 midnight? (18 hours)

Hours

31	a. Work (occupation)	_____
32-33	b. Sleep	_____
34	c. Work around the house	_____
35-36	d. Leisure activities	_____
37	e. Personal grooming	_____
38	f. Other	_____

7a. Do you work with any youth programs?

    39   1 ☐ No (If no, continue to 8)

         2 ☐ Yes

b. If **yes,** which ones? (check all that apply)

40 ☐ Scouting for boys   44-7 ☐ Other (List) ___

41 ☐ Scouting for girls   _____

42 ☐ 4–H   _____

43 ☐ Y Indian Guides   _____

8. Which of the following items of recreational equipment do you own? (Check all that apply)

48 ☐ Power boat   54 ☐ Golf clubs

49 ☐ Sail boat   55 ☐ Tennis racket

50 ☐ Canoe   56 ☐ Tent and other camping gear

51 ☐ Outboard motor   57 ☐ Camera

52 ☐ Shotgun or rifle   58 ☐ Toboggan or sled

53 ☐ Bow and arrow   59 ☐ None

60 Other_____   62 _____

61   _____   63 _____

9. To which outdoor organizations do you belong? (Check all that apply)

64 ☐ Audubon Society   67 ☐ Sportsmens Club

65 ☐ Izaak Walton League   68 ☐ Garden Club

66 ☐ Outboard Boat Club   69 ☐ None

70-3 ☐ Other (List) _____   _____

                    _____   _____

HEAD OF HOUSEHOLD:

10. 46-47 Age _____

11. 48 1 ☐ Male   2 ☐ Female

Please answer the following for each activity in which the head of the household
participates in a 30 day period and during the proper season.

12. Do you:

	Not at all	Approximate number of days in 30 day period	13. With whom				14. Where (most often)							
			Alone	Family or Friends	Organized Group		Lake	River	Creek			Name of Facility	State	
a. Go power boating?	49-50 ☐ 00	51 →	☐ 1	☐ 2	☐ 3	→ 52	☐ 1	☐ 2	☐ 3		53-54	55		
b. Go sailing?	56-57 ☐ 00	58 →	☐ 1	☐ 2	☐ 3	→ 59	☐ 1	☐ 2	☐ 3		60-61	62		
c. Canoe?	63-64 ☐ 00	65 →	☐ 1	☐ 2	☐ 3	→ 66	☐ 1	☐ 2	☐ 3		67-68	69		
									Pool					
d. Swim?	70-71 ☐ 00	72 →	☐ 1	☐ 2	☐ 3	→ 73	☐ 1	☐ 2	☐ 3	☐ 4	74-75	76		
e. Fish?	77-78 ☐ 00	79 →	☐ 1	☐ 2	☐ 3	→ 80	☐ 1	☐ 2	☐ 3		8-9	10		
f. Waterski?	11-12 ☐ 00	13 →	☐ 1	☐ 2	☐ 3	→ 14	☐ 1	☐ 2	☐ 3		15-16	17		

	Not at all	days	Alone	Family or Friends	Organized Group		Big Game	Small Game	Water Fowl		Public Area (check one)	Private Area	
g. Hunt (firearm)?	18-19 ☐ 00	20 →	☐ 1	☐ 2	☐ 3	→ 21	☐ 1	22 ☐	23 ☐	→ 24	☐ 1	☐ 2	
h. Hunt (bow and arrow)?	25-26 ☐ 00	27 →	☐ 1	☐ 2	☐ 3	→ 28	☐ 1	29 ☐	30 ☐	→ 31	☐ 1	☐ 2	
i. Target or trap shoot?	32-33 ☐ 00	34 →	☐ 1	☐ 2	☐ 3	→ 35					☐ 1	☐ 2	

	Not at all	days	Alone	Family or Friends	Organized Group		Developed Area	Wilderness or Remote Area		Public Area (check one)	Private Area	
j. Go camping (overnight)?	36-37 ☐ 00	38 →	☐ 1	☐ 2	☐ 3	→ 39	☐ 1	☐ 2		☐ 1	☐ 2	
k. Picnic?	40-41 ☐ 00	42 →	☐ 1	☐ 2	☐ 3	→ 43	☐ 1	☐ 2		☐ 1	☐ 2	

	Not at all	days	Alone	Family or Friends	Organized Group		Public Area (check one)	Private Area	
l. Walk or hike for pleasure?	44-45 ☐ 00	46 →	☐ 1	☐ 2	☐ 3	→ 47	☐ 1	☐ 2	
m. Go horseback riding?	48-49 ☐ 00	50 →	☐ 1	☐ 2	☐ 3	→ 51	☐ 1	☐ 2	
n. Play team sports?	52-53 ☐ 00	54 →	☐ 1	☐ 2	☐ 3	→ 55	☐ 1	☐ 2	
o. Golf?	56-57 ☐ 00	58 →	☐ 1	☐ 2	☐ 3	→ 59	☐ 1	☐ 2	
p. Play tennis?	60-61 ☐ 00	62 →	☐ 1	☐ 2	☐ 3	→ 63	☐ 1	☐ 2	
q. Go driving for pleasure?	64-65 ☐ 00	66 →	☐ 1	☐ 2	☐ 3				
r. Go bicycling?	67-68 ☐ 00	69 →	☐ 1	☐ 2	☐ 3				

15. 70-71 ☐ No spouse (If none skip to next page)   Age of Spouse _____

Please answer the following for each activity in which the spouse participates.

16. Do you: **17. With whom**   **18. Where** (most often)

	Approximate number of days in 30 day period	Not at all	Alone	Family or Friends	Organized Group	Lake	River	Creek			Name of Facility	State
a. Go power boating?	72-73	00	74 ☐1	☐2	75 ☐3	☐1	☐2	☐3			76-77	78
b. Go sailing?	79-80	00	8 ☐1	☐2	9 ☐3	☐1	☐2	☐3			10-11	12
c. Canoe?	13-14	00	15 ☐1	☐2	16 ☐3	☐1	☐2	☐3			17-18	19
d. Swim?	20-21	00	22 ☐1	☐2	23 ☐3	☐1	☐2	☐3	Pool 4☐		24-25	26
e. Fish?	27-28	00	29 ☐1	☐2	30 ☐3	☐1	☐2	☐3			31-32	33
f. Waterski?	34-35	00	36 ☐1	☐2	37 ☐3	☐1	☐2	☐3			38-39	40

						Big Game	Small Game	Water Fowl	
g. Hunt (firearm)?	41-42	00	43 ☐1	☐2	43 ☐3	44 ☐	45 ☐	46 ☐ — 47 ☐1
h. Hunt (bow and arrow?)	48-49	00	50 ☐1	☐2	☐3	51 ☐	52 ☐	53 ☐ — 54 ☐1
i. Target or trap shoot?	55-56	00	57 ☐1	☐2	☐3			58 ☐1

Developed Area / Wilderness or Remote Area (check one)

	Approximate number of days	Not at all	Alone	Family or Friends	Organized Group	Developed Area	Wilderness or Remote Area
j. Go camping (overnight)?	59-60	00	61 ☐1	☐2	☐3	62 ☐1	☐2
k. Picnic?	63-64	00	65 ☐1	☐2	☐3	66 ☐1	☐2

Public Area / Private Area (check one)

	Approximate number of days	Not at all	Alone	Family or Friends	Organized Group	Public Area	Private Area
l. Walk or hike for pleasure?	67-68	00	69 ☐1	☐2	☐3	70 ☐1	☐2
m. Go horseback riding?	71-72	00	73 ☐1	☐2	☐3	74 ☐1	☐2
n. Play team sports?	75-76	00	77 ☐1	☐2	☐3	78 ☐1	☐2
o. Golf?	79-80	00	8 ☐1	☐2	☐3	9 ☐1	☐2
p. Play tennis?	10-11	00	12 ☐1	☐2	☐3	13 ☐1	☐2
q. Go driving for pleasure?	14-15	00	16 ☐1	☐2	☐3		
r. Go bicycling?	17-18	00	19 ☐1	☐2	☐3		

OLDEST CHILD (Living at home)

19. 20-21 ☐ None (If none skip to page 7) Age of child _____ (living at home) participates.

20. 22 ☐₁ Male ☐₂ Female

Please answer the following for each activity in which the oldest child

21. Do you:

22. With whom

23. Where (most often)

	Not at all	Approximate number of days in 30 day period	Alone	Family or Friends	Organized Group	Lake	River	Creek		Name of Facility	State
a. Go power boating? 23-24	☐ 00	⟶ 25	☐ 1	☐ 2	☐₃ ⟶ 26	☐ 1	☐ 2	☐ 3		27-28	29
b. Go sailing? 30-31	☐ 00	⟶ 32	☐ 1	☐ 2	☐₃ ⟶ 33	☐ 1	☐ 2	☐ 3		34-35	36
c. Canoe? 37-38	☐ 00	⟶ 39	☐ 1	☐ 2	☐₃ ⟶ 40	☐ 1	☐ 2	☐ 3		41-42	43
d. Swim? 44-45	☐ 00	⟶ 46	☐ 1	☐ 2	☐₃ ⟶ 47	☐ 1	☐ 2	☐ 3	Pool ☐ 4 48-49	50
e. Fish? 51-52	☐ 00	⟶ 53	☐ 1	☐ 2	☐₃ ⟶ 54	☐ 1	☐ 2	☐ 3		55-56	57
f. Waterski? 58-59	☐ 00	⟶ 60	☐ 1	☐ 2	☐₃ ⟶ 61	☐ 1	☐ 2	☐ 3		62-63	64

						Big Game	Small Game	Water Fowl	Developed Area	Wilderness or Remote Area
									(check one)	
g. Hunt (firearm)? 65-66	☐ 00	⟶ 67	☐ 1	☐ 2	☐ 3	☐ 68	☐ 69	☐ 70 ⟶ 71		
h. Hunt (bow and arrow)? 72-73	☐ 00	⟶ 74	☐ 1	☐ 2	☐ 3	☐ 75	☐ 76	☐ 77 ⟶ 78		
i. Target or trap shoot? 79-80	☐ 00	⟶ 8	☐ 1 ☐	☐ 2	☐ 3 ⟶ 9					

						Public Area	Private Area
						(check one)	
j. Go camping (overnight)? 10-11	☐ 00	⟶ 12	☐ 1	☐ 2	☐₃ ⟶ 13	☐ 1	☐ 2
k. Picnic? 14-15	☐ 00	⟶ 16	☐ 1	☐ 2	☐₃ ⟶ 17	☐ 1	☐ 2

						Public Area	Private Area
						(check one)	
l. Walk or hike for pleasure? 18-19	☐ 00	⟶ 20	☐ 1	☐ 2	☐₃ ⟶ 21	☐ 1	☐ 2
m. Go horseback riding? 22-23	☐ 00	⟶ 24	☐ 1	☐ 2	☐₃ ⟶ 25	☐ 1	☐ 2
n. Play team sports? 26-27	☐ 00	⟶ 28	☐ 1	☐ 2	☐₃ ⟶ 29	☐ 1	☐ 2
o. Golf? 30-31	☐ 00	⟶ 32	☐ 1	☐ 2	☐₃ ⟶ 33	☐ 1	☐ 2
p. Play tennis? 34-35	☐ 00	⟶ 36	☐ 1	☐ 2	☐₃ ⟶ 37	☐ 1	☐ 2
q. Go driving for pleasure? 38-39	☐ 00	⟶ 40	☐ 1	☐ 2	☐ 3		
r. Go bicycling? 41-42	☐ 00	⟶ 43	☐ 1	☐ 2	☐ 3		

SECOND OLDEST CHILD (Living at home)

24. **44-45** □ None (If none skip to page 7) Age of child _____

25. **46** 1□ Male 2□ Female

26. Please answer the following for each activity in which the second oldest child (living at home) participates.

Do you:

	Not at all (00)	Approximate number of days in 30 day period	27. With whom — Alone (1)	Family or Friends (2)	Organized Group (3)	28. Where (most often) — Lake (1)	River (2)	Creek (3)	Name of Facility	State
a. Go power boating?	47-48	49			50			51-52	53	
b. Go sailing?	54-55	56			57			58-59	60	
c. Canoe?	61-62	63			64			65-66	67	
d. Swim?	68-69	70			71		Pool 4		72-73	74
e. Fish?	75-76	77			78			79-80	8	
f. Waterski?	9-10	11			12			13-14	15	

	Not at all (00)	Approximate number of days	Alone (1)	Family or Friends (2)	Organized Group (3)	Big Game (1)	Small Game (2)	Water Fowl
g. Hunt (firearm)?	16-17	18			19	20	21	22
h. Hunt (bow and arrow)?	23-24	25			26	27	28	29
i. Target or trap shoot?	30-31	32			33			

	Not at all (00)	Approximate number of days	Alone (1)	Family or Friends (2)	Organized Group (3)	Developed Area (1)	Wilderness or Remote Area (2) (check one)	Public Area (1)	Private Area (2) (check one)
j. Go camping (overnight)?	34-35	36			37				
k. Picnic?	38-39	40			41				

	Not at all (00)	Approximate number of days	Alone (1)	Family or Friends (2)	Organized Group (3)	Public Area (1)	Private Area (2) (check one)
l. Walk or hike for pleasure?	42-43	44			45		
m. Go horseback riding?	46-47	48			49		
n. Play team sports?	50-51	52			53		
o. Golf?	54-55	56			57		
p. Play tennis?	58-59	60			61		
q. Go driving for pleasure?	62-63	64					
r. Go bicycling?	65-66	67					

29. Which words best describe **LaSalle County** as a whole (not your own geographic location)?

Place a check in the square according to the best description.

70 a. 1☐————————2☐————————3☐————————4☐————————5☐
        Flat land   **Rolling**   **Hilly**

71 b. 1☐————————2☐————————3☐————————4☐————————5☐
        Cornfields   **Pasture**   **Woodlands**

72 c. 1☐————————2☐————————3☐————————4☐————————5☐
        Many rivers & creeks   **Few rivers & creeks**

73 d. 1☐————————2☐————————3☐————————4☐————————5☐
        Many lakes & ponds   **Few lakes & ponds**

74 e. 1☐————————2☐————————3☐————————4☐————————5☐
        Scenic   **Ugly**

75 f. 1☐————————2☐————————3☐————————4☐————————5☐
        Obvious planning   **No planning**

76 g. 1☐————————2☐————————3☐————————4☐————————5☐
        Sound use of natural resources   **Extreme waste**

77 h. 1☐————————2☐————————3☐————————4☐————————5☐
        Clean rivers   **Heavy pollution**

78 i. 1☐————————2☐————————3☐————————4☐————————5☐
        Clean air   **Heavy pollution**

30. What would you take a visitor from another state or country to see on a drive through the LaSalle countryside?

79-80 _____

_____

31. What do you like least about the countryside of LaSalle County? _____

    8-9   _____

            _____

32. Now we would like to know how you feel regarding the function of a Conservation District and other related items. Here are a few statements. Check the box which corresponds to how **you feel**. (Answer every question as best you can.)

	Completely Disagree	Partially Disagree	Partially Agree	Completely Agree
10 a. The conservation district should purchase lands and leave them natural for wildlife refuges, nature study, and scenic enjoyment	1 ☐	2 ☐	3 ☐	4 ☐
11 b. The conservation district should acquire lands and preserve them in a completely undisturbed state	1 ☐	2 ☐	3 ☐	4 ☐
12 c. The conservation district should develop facilities such as swimming areas, campgrounds, marinas, golf courses, etc., on the lands it acquires ..	1 ☐	2 ☐	3 ☐	4 ☐
13 d. The conservation district should charge user-fees at its facilities..............	1 ☐	2 ☐	3 ☐	4 ☐
14 e. Fees should be higher for non-residents of LaSalle County.....................	1 ☐	2 ☐	3 ☐	4 ☐
15 f. Private enterprise can do a better job of developing such facilities as lodging, marinas, golf courses, etc..	1 ☐	2 ☐	3 ☐	4 ☐
16 g. Lands suitable for recreational use should be under public ownership............	1 ☐	2 ☐	3 ☐	4 ☐

17 h. Federal assistance should be sought to help pay for the acquisition and development of conservation district facilities............. 1☐　　2☐　　3☐　　4☐

18 i. The conservation district should assume the park and recreation function in parts of the county not served by an existing Park District or Recreation Commission.......... 1☐　　2☐　　3☐　　4☐

19 j. The conservation district should become involved in pollution control ...... 1☐　　2☐　　3☐　　4☐

20 k. The conservation district should become involved in lands which they do not own (through lease, easement, etc.) .... 1☐　　2☐　　3☐　　4☐

33. Here are some additional statements. Check the box which tells how **you feel** about each statement.

		Not True	**True**
21 a.	There are enough outdoor-oriented organizations in LaSalle County..................	1☐	2☐
22 b.	There are plenty of outdoor recreational facilities in LaSalle County	1☐	2☐
23 c.	The conservation district should hire personnel to conduct programs in outdoor education and recreation	1☐	2☐
24 d.	Borrowing money is an appropriate way for a conservation district to secure funds for the development of facilities ...,....................................	1☐	2☐
25 e.	I prefer to be more of a participant in leisure rather than a spectator................	1☐	2☐
26 f.	There should be more man made bodies of water in LaSalle County	1☐	2☐
27 g.	Children have adequate opportunities to learn about nature	1☐	2☐

34a. Should the conservation district provide outdoor recreation facilities on the lands it shall acquire?

₁ ☐ No (If no continue to 35)

28 ₂ ☐ Yes

b. If **yes,** which of the following? (check)

29 ☐ Picnic areas complete with shelter houses

30 ☐ Hiking trails

31 ☐ Bridle paths

32 ☐ Playground equipment in the picnic areas

33 ☐ Softball and baseball diamonds

34 ☐ Playfields that can be used for football, badminton, volleyball, croquet, or other similar games

35 ☐ Fishing and boating lakes

36 ☐ Natural swimming area with sand beach

37 ☐ Swimming pool

38 ☐ Golf course

39 ☐ Overnight lodging

40 ☐ Regulated hunting

41 ☐ Group camp areas

42 ☐ Archery and rifle ranges

43 ☐ Boat ramps

44 ☐ Nature centers

45 ☐ Winter sports such as ice skating, sledding and tobogganning

46 ☐ Tent and/or trailer campgrounds for short-term use (one week or less)

47 ☐ Tent and/or trailer campgrounds for long-term use (one week or longer)

48-49 Other:_____

50-51 _____

52-53 _____

Skip to next page

35a. Should the conservation district conduct organized programs on the lands it shall acquire?

1☐ No (If no continue to 36)

54 2☐ Yes

b. If **yes,** which of the following? (check all that apply)

55☐ Competitive sports

56☐ Handicrafts

57☐ Instructions in fishing, boating, swimming, etc.

58☐ Overnight group camping

59☐ Bicycle trips

60☐ Canoeing trips

61☐ Day camps

62☐ Outdoor education

63☐ Other (List)_____

_____

_____

_____

36a. Do you go out occasionally on overnight camping trips?

1☐ No (If no continue to 37)

64 2☐ Yes

b. If **yes,** which type of campground do you prefer?

65 1☐ Primitive type with no marked sites where you set up at random within a specified area.

2☐ Primitive type with marked sites including driveway and picnic table, pit toilets, hand pumped wells, and no electrical outlets.

3☐ Improved type with marked sites including driveway and picnic table, flush toilets, running water, shower and laundry facilities, and electrical outlets.

37. Would you support a network of bicycle trails that connect the major population centers in the county with the Conservation District's properties and possibly other public recreational areas?

66 1☐ No   2☐ Yes

Please answer the following questions for **yourself** even though you are included earlier.

8-9 38. What is your age? _____

10 39. Are you: 1☐ Male?   2☐ Female?

11 40. Are you: 1☐ Married?
                    2☐ Single (never married)?
                    3☐ Divorced or separated?
                    4☐ Widowed?

41. Are there children living at home for which you did not have an answer sheet for activity estimates?

   ☐ No (If no continue to 42)
12 2☐ Yes

13 a. Age of third child_____
14 b. Age of fourth child_____
15 c. Age of fifth child_____

42. How many years of education have **you** completed? (Circle the number of years.)

16-17 Grade school: 1   2   3   4   5   6   7   8

       High school: 9   10   11   12

       College: 1   2   3   4   5

43. What is the occupation of the **chief wage earner** of the household?

   18-19 _____

44. How much was earned by all the adult members of the household last year? (check one)
   20 1☐ Under $5,000   4☐ $11,000 to $13,999   7☐ $20,000 to $24,999
       2☐ $5,000 to $7,999   5☐ $14,000 to $16,999   8☐ $25,000 to $29,999
       3☐ $8,000 to $10,999   6☐ $17,000 to $19,999   9☐ $30,000 or more

45. How long have you lived in LaSalle County? (check one)
   21 1☐ less than 1 year   4☐ 3 - 4 years   7☐ 9 - 10 years
       2☐ 1 year   5☐ 5 - 6 years   8☐ 10 - 15 years
       3☐ 2 years   6☐ 7 - 8 years   9☐ over 15 years

46a. Are there properties or natural features in LaSalle County that **you feel** are worthy of preservation and which should be in public ownership?

22 1☐ No
    2☐ Yes

b. If **yes**, please name them

23-24 _____

       _____

       _____

Additional Comments:

APPENDIX 4 Selected Game Area Size Standards

Name	Dimensions of game areas	Use dimensions (linear feet)	Space required (square feet)
Archery	90'–300' in length	50 × 175 (min.)	8,750
	Targets 15' apart	50 × 400 (max.)	20,000
Badminton	17' × 44' (singles)	25 × 60	1,500
	20' × 44' (doubles)	30 × 60	1,800
Baseball	90' diamond	350 × 350 (average with hooded backstop)	122,500
		400 × 400 (without backstop)	160,000
Basketball	42' × 74' (min.)	60 × 100	6,000
	50' × 94' (max.)	(average)	
Boccie	8' × 62'	20 × 80	1,600
Clock Golf	20'–30' diameter	40 × 40	1,600
Croquet	41' × 85'	50 × 95	4,750
Curling	Tees 114' apart	25 × 160	4,000
Field hockey	150' × 270' (min.)	210 × 330	69,300
	180' × 300' (max.)	(average)	
Football	160' × 360'	200 × 420	84,000
Handball	20' × 34'	30 × 45	1,350
Horseshoes	Stakes 40' apart	12 × 52 (min.)	624
Lacrosse	180' × 330' (min.)	225 × 360	81,000
	210' × 330' (max.)	(average)	
Lawn bowling	14' × 110' (1 alley)	130 × 130	16,900
Shuffleboard	6' × 52'	10 × 60	600
Soccer	165' × 300' (min.)	225 × 360	81,000
	225' × 360' (max.)	(average)	
Softball	55' diamond	275 × 275 (min.)	75,625
Tennis	27' × 78' (singles)	50 × 120	6,000
	36' × 78' (doubles)	60 × 120	7,200
Volleyball	30' × 60'	45 × 80	3,600

APPENDIX 5   Selected Game Area Layout Diagrams

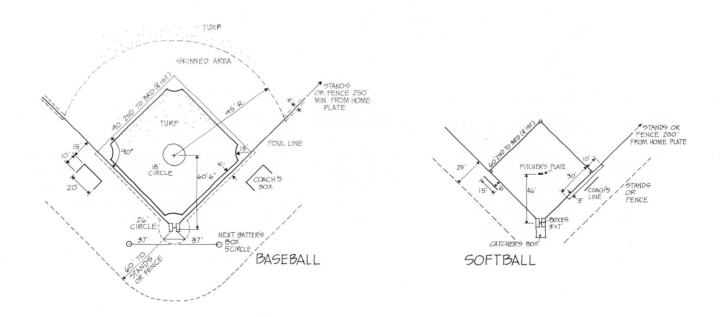

BASEBALL

SOFTBALL

TENNIS

SINGLES   DOUBLES

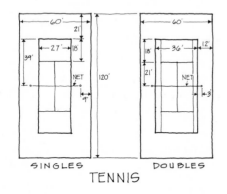

BASKETBALL

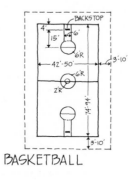

HANDBALL

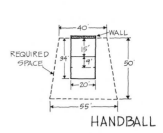

SCALE - BASEBALL, SOFTBALL, BASKETBALL,
TENNIS & HANDBALL ONLY

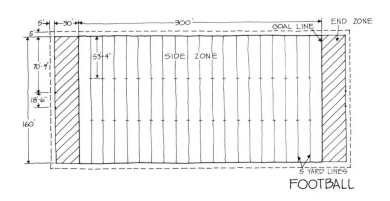

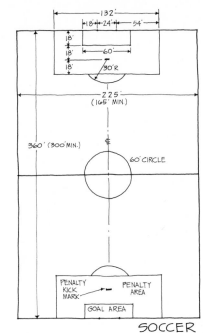

FOOTBALL

SOCCER

SCALE - FOOTBALL & SOCCER ONLY

APPENDIX 6   Responses of Selected Trees to Recreation Use

Abstracted from the Southeastern Forest Experiment Station Research Note 171, Asheville, North Carolina, February, 1962, the following represents the results of research conducted on forty-two camping and picnicking sites on the Cherokee, Nantahala, and Pisgah National Forests by the United States Department of Agriculture, Forest Service, Thomas H. Ripley, Project Director.

Data indicated little or no difference in damage, or in insect and disease problems related to size or dominance of the vegetation. Differences between species, however, were consistently large. The following conifers and hardwoods are listed in order of decreasing ability to withstand the impacts of recreation use, as gauged by disease infection, insect infestation, and decline.

Conifers
1. Shortleaf pine
2. Hemlock
3. White pine
4. Pitch pine
5. Virginia pine

Hardwoods

1. Hickories
2. Persimmon
3. Sycamore
4. White ash
5. Beech
6. Sassafrass
7. Buckeye
8. Yellow poplar
9. Dogwood
10. Blackgum
11. Yellow birch
12. Red maple
13. American holly
14. Sourwood
15. Black birch
16. White oaks
17. Black walnut
18. Red oak
19. Black locust
20. Magnolia
21. Black cherry
22. Blue beech

Conifers were clearly more susceptible to disease and insect attack than were hardwoods—with the possible exception of shortleaf pine and hemlock.

APPENDIX 7 Responses of Selected Soil Types to Recreation Use

The following are a few excerpts from *Soil Interpretations for Recreation*, prepared in 1969 by the United States Department of Agriculture, Soil Conservation Service for an Illinois region. The entire table contains ratings for hundreds of soil types.

Similar work has been done by the Soil Conservation Service for other regions, the ratings serving as preliminary information which may require further detailed on-site investigations on the part of the user. Where soil maps or interpretations such as these are not available, the designer must rely even more upon site observations, usually couching his inventory in such general terms as wet soil, fertile soil, rocky soil, etc., rather than the sophisticated soil-type labels indicated here.

TABLE 4. Soil Interpretations for Recreation for Major Land Resource Area_____ _____(Work Sheet)

Degree of Limitations and Soil Features Affecting Use*

Sheet _____ of _____

Soil type and phase†	Cottages and utility buildings	Intensive campsites	Picnic area	Intensive play areas	Trail and paths	Golf fairways
Ade loamy fine sand:						
0–2% slopes	Moderate (dr, bl)	Moderate (t, dr, bl)	Moderate (t, dr, bl)	Moderate (t, dr, bl)	Moderate (t, bl)	Severe (dr)
2–6% slopes	Moderate (dr, bl)	Moderate (t, dr, bl)	Moderate (t, dr, bl)	Moderate (t, s, dr, bl)	Moderate (t, bl)	Severe (dr)
6–12% slopes	Moderate (dr, bl)	Severe (t, e, s, dr, bl)	Moderate (t, e, s, dr, bl)	Severe (t, e, s, dr, bl)	Moderate (t, e, bl)	Severe (s, dr)
Alvin fine sandy loam:						
2–4% slopes	Slight	Slight	Slight	Moderate	Slight	Slight
4–7% slopes	Slight	Slight	Slight	Moderate (s)	Slight	Slight
7–12% slopes	Moderate (s)	Moderate (s)	Moderate (s)	Severe (s)	Slight	Moderate (s)
12–18% slopes	Severe (s)	Severe (s)	Severe (s)	Severe (s)	Moderate (s)	Severe (s)
18–30% slopes	Severe (s)	Severe (s)	Severe (s)	Severe (s)	Severe (s)	Severe (s)
Andres loam or silt loam:						
0–2% slopes	Moderate (w)	Moderate (w)	Moderate (w)	Moderate (w)	Moderate (w)	Moderate (w)
2–4% slopes	Moderate (w)	Moderate (w)	Moderate (w)	Moderate (s, w)	Moderate (w)	Moderate (w)
Aptakasic silt loam:						
0–2% slopes	Moderate (w)	Moderate (d)	Moderate (d)	Moderate (d)	Moderate (d)	Moderate (d)
Ashkum silty clay loam:						
0–3% slopes	Severe (w, f)	Severe (w, f, t)	Severe (w, f, t)	Severe (w, f, t)	Severe (w, f, t)	Severe (w, f)
Ayr loam, fine sandy loam, or sandy loam:						
0–2% slopes	Slight	Slight	Slight	Slight	Slight	Slight
2–6% slopes	Slight	Slight	Slight	Moderate (s)	Slight	Slight
6–12% slopes	Moderate (s)	Moderate (s)	Moderate (s)	Severe (s)	Slight	Moderate (s)

* Soils are rated on the basis of four classes of soil limitations: *Slight*—relatively free of limitations or limitations are easily overcome; *Moderate*—limitations need to be recognized, but can be overcome with good management and careful design; *Severe*—limitations severe enough to make use questionable; *Very Severe*—extreme measures are needed to overcome the limitations and usage generally is unsound or not practical.

Kind of limitation: b-bedrock depth; d-drainage; e-erosion; f-flooding or ponding; p-permeability; r-rockiness or stony; s-slope; t-texture of surface; w-watertable; i-inherent fertility; dr-drouthy; bl-blowing.

† Only slope phases are shown, unless the interpretations differ by erosion phases.

TABLE 4. Soil Interpretations for Recreation for Major Land Resource Area —(Work Sheet) (continued)

Degree of Limitations and Soil Features Affecting Use*

Soil type and phase†	Cottages and utility buildings	Intensive campsites	Picnic area	Intensive play areas	Trail and paths	Golf fairways
Aztalan loam:						
0–2% slopes	Moderate (w)	Moderate (w)	Moderate (w)	Moderate (w)	Moderate (w)	Moderate (w)
2–6% slopes	Moderate (w)	Moderate (w)	Moderate (w)	Moderate (s, w)	Moderate (w)	Moderate (w)
Beecher silt loam:						
1–4% slopes	Moderate (w)	Moderate (w, p)	Moderate (w, p)	Moderate (w, p, s)	Moderate (w)	Moderate (w)
4–7% slopes	Moderate (w)	Moderate (w, p)	Moderate (w, p)	Moderate (w, p, s)	Moderate (w)	Moderate (s, w)
Billett sandy loam:						
0–2% slopes	Slight	Slight	Slight	Slight	Slight	Slight to moderate (dr)
2–4% slopes	Slight	Slight	Slight	Moderate (s)	Slight	Slight to moderate (dr)
4–7% slopes	Slight	Slight	Slight	Moderate (s)	Slight	Moderate (s, dr)
7–12% slopes	Moderate (s)	Moderate (s)	Moderate (s)	Severe (s)	Slight	Moderate (s, dr)
Bloomfield fine sand and loamy fine sand:						
0–6% slopes	Moderate (dr, bl, i, s)	Moderate (t, dr, bl, i, s)	Moderate (t, dr, bl, i, s)	Moderate (t, bl, s)	Moderate (t)	Severe (t, dr, i, s)
6–12% slopes	Moderate (dr, bl, i, s)	Moderate (t, dr, bl, i, s)	Moderate (t, dr, bl, i, s)	Severe (t, dr, bl, i, s)	Moderate (t)	Severe (t, dr, i, s)
12–18% slopes	Severe (s, dr, bl, i)	Severe (s, t, dr, bl, i)	Severe (s, t, dr, bl, i)	Severe (t, dr, bl, i, s)	Moderate (s, t)	Severe (t, dr, i, s)
18+%	Severe (s, dr, bl, i)	Severe (s, t, dr, bl, i)	Severe (s, t, dr, bl, i)	Severe (t, dr, bl, i, s)	Severe (s, t)	Severe (t, dr, i, s)
Blount silt loam:						
0–2% slopes	Moderate (w)	Moderate (w, p)	Moderate (w, p)	Moderate (w, p)	Moderate (w)	Moderate (w)
2–6% slopes	Moderate (w)	Moderate (w, p)	Moderate (w, p)	Moderate (w, p, s)	Moderate (w)	Moderate (w)
Brenton silt loam:						
0–2% slopes	Moderate (w)	Moderate (w)	Moderate (w)	Moderate (w)	Moderate (w)	Moderate (w)
2–4% slopes	Moderate (w)	Moderate (w)	Moderate (w)	Moderate (s, w)	Moderate (w)	Moderate (w)
Brooklyn silt loam:						
0–2% slopes	Severe (w, f, d)	Severe (w, f, d)	Severe (w, f, d)	Severe (w, p, f, d)	Severe (w, f)	Severe (w, f, d)
Bryce silty clay loam:						
0–2% slopes	Severe (w, f, d)	Severe (p, w, f, d, t)	Severe (p, w, f, d, t)	Severe (p, w, f, d, t)	Severe (p, w, f, t)	Severe (p, w, f, d, t)
Camden silt loam:						
0–2% slopes	Slight	Slight	Slight	Slight	Slight	Slight
2–4% slopes	Slight	Slight	Slight	Moderate (s)	Slight	Slight
4–7% slopes	Moderate (s)	Slight	Slight	Moderate (s)	Slight	Slight
7–12% slopes	Moderate (s)	Moderate (s)	Moderate (s)	Severe (s)	Moderate (s)	Moderate (s)
12–18% slopes	Severe (s)	Severe (s)	Severe (s)	Severe (s)	Severe (s)	Severe (s)
18+% slopes	Severe (s)	Severe (s)	Severe (s)	Severe (s)	Severe (s)	Severe (s)

Casco loam or silt loam:						
0–2% slopes	Slight (dr)	Slight (dr)	Slight (dr)	Slight (dr)	Slight (dr)	Slight
2–6% slopes	Slight (dr)	Slight (dr)	Slight (dr)	Moderate (s, dr)	Slight (dr)	Slight
6–12% slopes	Moderate (s, dr)	Moderate (s)	Moderate (s, dr)	Severe (s, dr)	Slight (dr)	Moderate (s, dr)
12–30% slopes	Severe (s, dr)	Severe (s)	Severe (s, dr)	Severe (s, dr)	Moderate (s)	Severe (s, dr, e)
Catlin silt loam:						
0–2% slopes	Slight	Slight	Slight	Slight	Slight	Slight
2–6% slopes	Slight	Slight	Slight	Moderate (s)	Slight	Slight
6–12% slopes	Moderate (s)	Moderate (s)	Moderate (s)	Severe (s)	Slight	Moderate (s)
Chalmers silty clay loam:						
0–2% slopes	Severe (w, f, d, t)	Severe (w, f, d, t)	Severe (w, f, d, t)	Severe (w, f, d, t)	Severe (w, f, d, t)	Severe (w, f, d, t)
Channahon silt loam to loam:						
2–4% slopes	Severe (b)	Slight	Slight	Severe (b, s)	Slight	Slight (b)
4–7% slopes	Severe (b)	Slight	Slight	Severe (b, s)	Slight	Moderate (s, b)
Chatsworth silt loam:						
7–12% slopes	Severe (s, e)	Severe (p, e, s)	Severe (e, s, i)	Severe (s, e, p, i)	Moderate (p)	Severe (e, s, i)
12–18% slopes	Severe (s, e)	Severe (p, e, s)	Severe (e, s, i)	Severe (s, e, p, i)	Moderate (p)	Severe (e, s, i)
18–30+% slopes	Severe (s, e)	Severe (p, e, s)	Severe (e, s, i)	Severe (s, e, p, i)	Severe (s)	Severe (e, s, i)
Clarence silty clay loam:						
0–12% slopes, slight and moderate eroded	Moderate (w, d)	Moderate (w, d)	Moderate (w, d)	Moderate (w, p, d, s)	Moderate (w, p)	Moderate (w, p, dr, d)
2–12% slopes, severe eroded	Severe (w, dr)	Severe (t, p, w, dr, d)	Severe (t, p, w, dr, d)	Severe (s, p, w, t, dr, d)	Severe (t, p, w)	Severe (w, dr, d)

* Soils are rated on the basis of four classes of soil limitations: *Slight*—relatively free of limitations or limitations are easily overcome; *Moderate*—limitations need to be recognized, but can be overcome with good management and careful design; *Severe*—limitations severe enough to make use questionable; *Very Severe*—extreme measures are needed to overcome the limitations and usage generally is unsound or not practical.

Kind of limitation: b-bedrock depth; d-drainage; e-erosion; f-flooding or ponding; p-permeability; r-rockiness or stony; s-slope; t-texture of surface; w-watertable; i-inherent fertility; dr-drouthy; bl-blowing.

† Only slope phases are shown, unless the interpretations differ by erosion phases.

Sheet____of____

TABLE 4. *Soil Interpretations for Recreation for Major Land Resource Area*

Degree of Limitations and Soil Features Affecting Use*

Soil type and phase†	Cottages and utility buildings	Intensive campsites	Picnic area	Intensive play areas	Trail and paths	Golf fairways
Colwood silt loam:						
0–3% slopes	Severe (w, d)	Severe (w, d)	Severe (w, d)	Severe (w, d)	Severe (w, d)	Severe (w, d)
Corwin loam or silt loam:						
0–2% slopes	Slight	Slight	Slight	Slight	Slight	Slight
2–6% slopes	Slight	Slight	Slight	Moderate (s)	Slight	Slight
6–12% slopes	Moderate (s)	Moderate (s)	Moderate (s)	Severe (s)	Slight	Moderate (s)
Dana silt loam:						
0–2% slopes	Slight	Slight	Slight	Slight	Slight	Slight
2–6% slopes	Slight	Slight	Slight	Moderate (s)	Slight	Slight
Darroch silt loam or loam:						
0–2% slopes	Moderate (w, d)	Moderate (w, d)	Moderate (w, d)	Moderate (w, d)	Moderate (w, d)	Moderate (w, d)
Deardurff loam or fine sandy loam:						
0–2% slopes	Slight	Slight	Slight	Slight	Slight	Slight
2–6% slopes	Slight	Slight	Slight	Moderate (s, dr)	Slight	Slight
Del Rey silt loam:						
0–4% slopes	Moderate (w)	Moderate (w, p)	Moderate (w, p)	Moderate (w, p, s)	Moderate (w)	Moderate (w)
Dickinson sandy loam:						
0–2% slopes	Slight	Slight	Slight	Slight	Slight	Slight
2–6% slopes	Slight	Slight	Slight	Moderate (s, dr)	Slight	Slight
Dodge silt loam:						
2–7% slopes	Slight	Slight	Slight	Moderate (s)	Slight	Slight
7–12% slopes	Moderate (s)	Moderate (s)	Moderate (s)	Severe (s)	Slight	Moderate (s)
12–30% slopes	Severe (s)	Severe (s)	Severe (s)	Severe (s)	Moderate (s)	Severe (s)
Dorchester silt loam:						
0–2% slopes	Severe (f, w)	Severe (f, w)	Moderate (f, w)	Severe (f, w)	Moderate (f, w)	Moderate (f, w)
Dresden loam or silt loam:						
0–2% slopes	Slight	Slight	Slight	Slight	Slight	Slight
2–4% slopes	Slight	Slight	Slight	Moderate (s)	Slight	Slight
4–7% slopes	Slight	Slight	Slight	Moderate (s)	Slight	Slight
Drummer silty clay loam:						
0–2% slopes	Severe (w, f)	Severe (w, f, t)	Severe (w, f, t)	Severe (w, f, t)	Severe (w, f, t)	Severe (w, f)

Soil and slope						
Dupage silt loam:						
0–2% slopes	Severe (f, w)	Severe (f, w)	Moderate to severe	Severe (f, w)	Moderate (f, w)	Severe (f, w)
2–4% slopes	Severe (f, w)	Severe (f)	Moderate (f)	Severe (f, s)	Moderate (f)	Moderate (f)
Elliott silt loam or silty clay loam:						
0–2% slopes	Moderate (w)	Moderate (w, p)	Moderate (w, p)	Moderate (w, p)	Moderate (w)	Moderate (w)
2–6% slopes	Moderate (w)	Moderate (w, p)	Moderate (w, p)	Moderate (w, p, s)	Moderate (w)	Moderate (w)
Ellison silt loam:						
0–2% slopes	Slight	Slight	Slight	Slight	Slight	Slight
2–4% slopes	Slight	Slight	Slight	Moderate (s)	Slight	Slight
4–7% slopes	Slight	Slight	Slight	Moderate (s)	Slight	Slight
Elston sandy loam or loam:						
0–2% slopes	Slight (dr)	Slight (dr)	Slight (dr)	Slight (dr)	Slight (dr)	Moderate (s, dr)
2–6% slopes	Slight (dr)	Slight (dr)	Slight (dr)	Moderate (s, dr)	Slight (dr)	Moderate (s, dr)
6–12% slopes	Moderate (s, dr)	Moderate (s)	Moderate (s, dr)	Severe (s, dr)	Slight (dr)	Moderate (s, dr)
Epworth fine sandy loam:						
0–2% slopes	Slight (dr)	Slight (dr)	Slight (dr)	Slight (dr)	Slight	Slight (dr)
2–4% slopes	Slight (dr)	Slight (dr)	Slight (dr)	Moderate (s, bl, dr)	Slight	Slight (dr)
Flanagan silt loam:						
0–2% slopes	Moderate (w)	Moderate (w)	Moderate (w)	Moderate (w)	Moderate (w)	Moderate (w)
2–6% slopes	Moderate (w)	Moderate (w)	Moderate (w)	Moderate (s, w)	Moderate (w)	Moderate (w)
Fox silt loam or loam:						
0–2% slopes	Slight	Slight	Slight	Slight	Slight	Slight
2–6% slopes	Slight	Slight	Slight	Moderate (s)	Slight	Slight
6–12% slopes	Moderate (s)	Moderate (s)	Mode ate (s)	Severe (s)	Slight	Moderate (s)
12–18% slopes	Severe (s)	Severe (s)	Severe (s)	Severe (s)	Moderate (s)	Severe (s)
Frankfort silt loam to silty clay loam:						
2–4% slopes	Moderate (w)	Moderate (p, w)	Moderate (p, w)	Moderate (s, .p, w)	Moderate (p, w, s)	Moderate (w, e)
4–7% slopes	Moderate (w)	Moderate (p, w)	Moderate (p, w)	Moderate (s, p, w)	Moderate (p, w, e)	Moderate (s, e, w)

Sheet _____ of _____

TABLE 4. Soil Interpretations for Recreation for Major Land Resource Area _____

Degree of Limitations and Soil Features Affecting Use*

Soil type and phase†	Cottages and utility buildings	Intensive campsites	Picnic area	Intensive play areas	Trail and paths	Golf fairways
Granby fine sandy loam:						
0–3% slopes	Severe (w, d)	Severe (w, d)	Severe (w, d)	Severe (w, d)	Moderate to severe (w, d)	Severe (w, d)
Grays silt loam:						
2–4% slopes	Slight	Slight	Slight	Moderate (s)	Slight	Slight
Harpster silt loam or loam:						
0–4% slopes	Severe (w, f)	Severe (w, f)	Severe (w, f)	Severe (w, f)	Severe (w, f)	Severe (w, f)
Harpster silty clay or loam:						
0–2% slopes	Severe (w, f)	Severe (w, f)	Severe (w, f)	Severe (w, f)	Severe (w, f)	Severe (w, f)
Harvard silt loam:						
0–2% slopes	Slight	Slight	Slight	Slight	Slight	Slight
2–4% slopes	Slight	Slight	Slight	Moderate (s)	Slight	Slight
4–7% slopes	Slight	Slight	Slight	Moderate (s)	Slight	Slight
7–12% slopes	Moderate (s)	Moderate (s)	Moderate (s)	Severe (s)	Slight	Moderate (s)
12–18% slopes	Severe (s)	Severe (s)	Severe (s)	Severe (s)	Moderate (s)	Severe (s)
Hebron loam:						
0–2% slopes	Slight	Slight	Slight	Slight	Slight	Slight
2–6% slopes	Slight	Slight	Slight	Moderate (s)	Slight	Slight
6–12% slopes	Moderate (s)	Moderate (s)	Moderate (s)	Severe (s)	Slight	Moderate (s)
Hannepin loam or silt loam:						
4–7% slopes	Slight	Slight	Slight	Moderate (s)	Slight	Slight
7–12% slopes	Moderate (s)	Moderate (s)	Moderate (s)	Severe (s)	Slight	Moderate (s)
12–18% slopes	Severe (s)	Severe (s)	Severe (s)	Severe (s)	Moderate (s)	Severe (s)
18+% slopes	Severe (s)	Severe (s)	Severe (s)	Severe (s)	Severe (s)	Severe (s)
Herbert silt loam:						
0–2% slopes	Moderate (w)	Moderate (w)	Moderate (w)	Moderate (w)	Moderate (w)	Moderate (w)
2–4% slopes	Moderate (w)	Moderate (w)	Moderate (w)	Moderate (s, w)	Moderate (w)	Moderate (w)

Sheet _____ of _____

*Soils are rated on the basis of four classes of soil limitations: *Slight*—relatively free of limitations or limitations are easily overcome; *Moderate*—limitations need to be recognized, but can be overcome with good management and careful design; *Severe*—limitations severe enough to make use questionable; *Very Severe*—extreme measures are needed to overcome the limitations and usage generally is unsound or not practical.

Kind of limitation: b-bedrock depth; d-drainage; e-erosion; f-flooding or ponding; p-permeability; r-rockiness or stony; s-slope; t-texture of surface; w-watertable; i-inherent fertility; dr-drouthy; bl-blowing.

†Only slope phases are shown, unless the interpretations differ by erosion phases.

 *Bibliography*

The numbers in parentheses which follow each citation refer to the chapters in this book which the reference most directly augments. Within these parentheses, an asterisk * indicates that the reference contains information related to the natural resource aspects of park system planning.

Aaron, David, with Bonnie P. Winawer: *Child's Play: A Creative Approach to Playscapes for Today's Children,* Harper & Row, Publishers, Incorporated, New York, 1965. (2,3)

Allen, Marjorie: *Design for Play,* E. T. Hawn and Company, Ltd., London, 1962. (2,3)

―――: *New Playgrounds,* E. T. Hawn and Company, Ltd., London, 1964. (2,3)

―――: *Planning for Play,* The M.I.T. Press, Cambridge, Mass., 1968. (2,3)

American Camping Association: *Tent and Trailer Sites,* Bradford Woods, Ind., 1962. (4)

Appleyard, Donald, Kevin Lynch, and John R. Myer: *The View from the Road,* The M.I.T. Press, Cambridge, Mass., 1964. (2)

Ardrey, Robert: *The Territorial Imperative,* Atheneum Publishers, New York, 1966. (2)

Arnold, Serena E.: *Trends in Consolidation of Parks and Recreation: Including Pros and Cons,* American Institute of Park Executives Management Aids Bulletin, no. 41, Wheeling, W.Va., 1964. (1)

Blake, Peter: *God's Own Junkyard: The Planned Deterioration of America's Landscape,* Holt, Rinehart, and Winston, Inc. New York, 1964. (1)

Brown, Joe, and David G. Wright: *Marinas: A Guide to Their Development for Park and Recreation Departments,* American Institute of Park Executives Management Aids Bulletin, no. 54, Wheeling, W.Va., 1965. (4)

Butler, George D.: *Introduction to Community Recreation,* McGraw-Hill Book Company, New York, 1959. (2,4)

————: *Recreation Areas: Their Design and Equipment,* The Ronald Press Company, New York, 1958. (2,4)

————: *Standards for Municipal Recreation Areas,* National Recreation Association, New York, 1962. (2,4)

Caskey, George B., and David G. Wright: *Coasting and Tobogganing Facilities,* National Recreation and Park Association Management Aids Bulletin, no. 62, Wheeling, W.Va., 1966. (4)

Chaney, Charles A.: *Marinas: Recommendations for Design, Construction, and Maintenance,* National Association of Engine and Boat Manufacturers, New York, 1961. (4)

Clawson, Marion: *Land and Water for Recreation,* Rand McNally & Company, Chicago, 1963. (1)

————: *Land for Americans,* Rand McNally & Company, Chicago, 1965. (1)

Connell, Edward A.: *Lawn Bowling: An Analysis of Public Operations,* American Institute of Park Executives Management Aids Bulletin, no. 10, Wheeling, W.Va., 1961. (4)

Cook, Walter L.: *Manual and Survey for Public Safety for Park and Recreation Departments,* American Institute of Park Executives Management Aids Bulletin, no. 20, Wheeling, W.Va., 1962. (4)

————: *Shooting Ranges: A Survey of and Manual for Park and/or Recreation Departments,* American Institute of Park Executives Management Aids Bulletin, no. 35, Wheeling, W.Va., 1964. (4)

Danford, Howard G.: *Recreation in the American Community,* Harper & Brothers, New York, 1953. (2,4)

Doell, Charles E.: *Elements of Park and Recreation Administration,* Burgess Publishing Company, Minneapolis, Minn., 1963. (1,2,4,6)

————, and Gerald B. Fitzgerald: *A Brief History of Parks and Recreation in the United States,* The Athletic Institute, Chicago, 1954. (1)

Douglass, Robert W.: *Forest Recreation,* Pergamon Press, New York, 1969. (4)

Dubos, René: *So Human an Animal: How We Are Shaped by Surroundings and Events,* Charles Scribner's Sons, New York, 1969. (2,3)

Dulles, Rhea D.: *A History of Recreation,* Meredith Publishing Company, Des Moines, Iowa, 1965. (1)

Eckbo, Garrett: *The Landscape We See,* McGraw-Hill Book Company, New York, 1969. (1,2,3,4,5,6,*)

————: *Urban Landscape Design,* McGraw-Hill Book Company, New York, 1964. (1,2,3,4,5,6)

Fabos, Julius Gy., Gordon T. Milde, and Michael Weinmayer: *Frederick Law Olmsted, Sr.: Founder of Landscape Architecture in America,* University of Massachusetts Press, Amherst, 1968. (1)

Fine, Albert: *Landscape into Cityscape: Frederick Law Olmsted's Plans for a Greater New York,* Cornell University Press, Ithaca, N.Y., 1968. (1)

Gabrielsen, M. Alexander, and Caswell M. Miles: *Sports and Recreation Facilities for School and Community,* Prentice-Hall, Inc., Englewood Cliffs, N.J., 1958. (4)

Hall, Edward T.: *The Hidden Dimension,* Doubleday & Company, Inc., Garden City, N.Y., 1966. (3)

————: *The Silent Language,* Doubleday & Company, Inc., Garden City, N.Y., 1959. (2)

Harvard University Landscape Architecture Research Office: *Three Approaches to Environmental Analysis,* The Conservation Foundation, Washington, D.C., 1967. (6,*)

Hittson, Hamilton, and Paul N. Jones: *Building and Programming Casting Pools,* American Institute of Park Executives Management Aids Bulletin, no. 12, Wheeling, W.Va., 1962. (4)

Holland, Roy (ed.): *Planning and Building the Golf Course,* National Golf Foundation, Inc., Chicago, 1959. (4)

Jarrell, Temple R.: *Horseshoe Pitching: A Guide to Court Layouts,* National Park and Recreation Association Management Aids Bulletin, no. 71, Wheeling, W.Va., 1967. (4)

Kotter, David H.: "Landscape Design Criteria for Ski Slope Development," master's thesis, University of Illinois, Urbana, 1967. (3,4)

LaGasse, Alfred B.: *Drag Strips, Why, When, and How: A Survey of Public Operations,* American Institute of Park Executives Management Aids Bulletin, no. 19, Wheeling, W.Va., 1962. (4)

——, and Walter L. Cook: *History of Parks and Recreation,* American Institute of Park Executives Management Aids Bulletin, no. 56, Wheeling, W.Va., 1965. (1)

Ledermann, Alfred, and Alfred Trachsel: *Creative Playgrounds and Recreation Centers,* Frederick A. Praeger, Inc., New York, 1968. (2,3)

Lewis, Philip H., Jr., and Associates: *Regional Design for Human Impact,* Thomas Printing and Publishing Company, Ltd., Kaukana, Wis., 1968. (*)

Lynch, Kevin: *Site Planning,* The M.I.T. Press, Cambridge, Mass., 1962. (2,3,4,5,6)

McHarg, Ian L.: *Design with Nature,* The Natural History Press, Garden City, N.Y., 1969. (1,2,3,4,6,*)

Moeller, John: *Standards for Outdoor Recreation Areas,* American Society of Planning Officials, Chicago, 1965. (2,4)

Molnar, Donald J.: "Physical Design Criteria for the Landscape Design of Pre-school Play Areas," master's thesis, University of Illinois, Urbana, 1964. (2,3,7)

Mott, William Penn, Jr.: *Creative Playground Equipment,* American Institute of Park Executives Management Aids Bulletin, no. 40, Wheeling, W.Va., 1964. (2)

Mueller, Eva, and Gerald Gurin: *Participation in Outdoor Recreation: Factors Affecting Demand Among American Adults,* Report to the Outdoor Recreation Resources Review Commission, Government Printing Office, Washington, D.C., 1962. (2)

National Facilities Conference: *Planning Facilities for Health, Physical Education, and Recreation,* The Athletic Institute, Chicago, 1962. (2,4,7)

Olgay, Victor: *Design with Climate,* Princeton University Press, Princeton, N.J., 1963. (4)

Park Association of New York, Inc.: *New Parks for New York,* New York, 1963. (1,7)

Purdue University, Cooperative Extension Service: *Guidelines for Developing Land for Outdoor Recreational Uses,* West Lafayette, Ind., 1963. (4,6)

Ramsey, Charles G., and Harold R. Sleeper: *Architectural Graphic Standards,* John Wiley & Sons, Inc., New York, 1956. (4)

Ripley, T. H.: *Tree and Shrub Response to Recreation Use,* U.S. Forest Service, Southeastern Forest Experiment Station, Research Note 171, Asheville, N.C., 1962. (4)

Rombold, Charles C.: *Guidelines for Campground Development,* American Institute of Park Executives Management Aids Bulletin, no. 34, Wheeling, W.Va., 1964. (4)

_____: *Natural Ice Skating Surfaces*, American Institute of Park Executives Management Aids Bulletin, no. 37, Wheeling, W.Va., 1964. (4)

_____: *Signs and Symbols for Park and Recreation Use*, American Institute of Park Executives Management Aids Bulletin, no. 39, Wheeling, W.Va., 1964. (4)

Rubenstein, Harvey M.: *A Guide to Site and Environmental Planning*, John Wiley & Sons, Inc., New York, 1969. (2,3,4,5,6)

Salomon, J. H.: *Campsite Development*, Girl Scouts of the United States of America Council Administrative Series, no. 5B, New York, 1959. (4)

Simonds, John O.: *Landscape Architecture: The Shaping of Man's Natural Environment*, McGraw-Hill Book Company, New York, 1961. (1,2,3,4,5,6)

Sommer, Robert: *Personal Space: The Behavioral Basis of Design*, Prentice-Hall, Inc., Englewood Cliffs, N.J., 1969. (2)

Stott, Charles C.: *Evaluating Water Based Recreation Facilities and Areas*, National Recreation and Park Association Management Aids Bulletin, no. 70, Wheeling, W.Va., 1967. (4)

Udall, Stewart L.: *The Quiet Crisis*, Holt, Rinehart, and Winston, Inc., New York, 1963. (1)

United States Department of Agriculture, Forest Service: *The American Outdoors: Management for Beauty and Use*, Misc. Publication #1000, 1965. (1,3,4)

United States Department of the Interior, Bureau of Outdoor Recreation: *Outdoor Recreation Space Standards*, 1967. (2,4)

_____, National Park Service: *Special Park Uses*, 1961. (2,4)

Van Meter, Jerry R.: *Master Plans for Park Sites*, University of Illinois Cooperative Extension Service, Urbana, 1969. (2,4,6)

Vollmer, Associates: *Parking for Recreation*, American Institute of Park Executives, Wheeling, W.Va., 1965. (4)

Weddle, A. E. (ed.): *Techniques of Landscape Architecture*, William Heinemann, Ltd., London, 1967. (2,3,4,5,6)

Whyte, William H.: *Cluster Development*, American Conservation Association, New York, 1964. (1,*)

_____: *The Last Landscape*, Doubleday & Company, Inc., Garden City, N.Y., 1968. (1,*)

Williams, Wayne R.: *Recreation Places*, Reinhold Publishing Corporation, New York, 1958. (2,3,4)

Wilson, George T.: *Vandalism: How to Stop It*, American Institute of Park Executives Management Aids Bulletin, ·no. 7, Wheeling, W.Va., 1961. (4)

Wisconsin, State of, Bureau of Recreation: *Recreation Site Evaluation*, Madison, Wis., 1968. (2,4,*)

Wright, David G.: *Public Beaches*, American Institute of Park Executives Management Aids Bulletin, no. 51, Wheeling, W.Va., 1965. (4)

Wyman, Donald: *Shrubs and Vines for American Gardens*, The Macmillan Company, New York, 1969. (4)

_____: *Trees for American Gardens*, The Macmillan Company, New York, 1959. (4)

Young Men's Christian Association National Commission on YMCA Camp Layouts, Buildings, and Facilities: *Developing Campsites and Facilities*, Association Press, New York, 1960. (4)

Index

Aesthetics (*see* Beauty)
Amphitheaters, 12, 14
Ardrey, Robert, 24
Automobiles (*see* Circulation systems)

Baseball diamonds, 16, 51, 58, 75, 110,
    112, 113, 164
Beauty, 31, 32, 137
    creating experiences, 37–49
    determining quality, 35, 36, 49–51, 53
Behavior:
    avoiding injury circumstances, 25, 26, 75
    challenge, 28, 75
    companionship, 26, 30
    design criteria, formulating, 29, 30
    empirical evidence, gathering, 25, 28–30
    freedom, 27, 69, 70, 132
    as influencing design, 23–30
    mental exercise, 8, 9, 27, 28

Behavior (*Cont.*):
    order, environmental, 36–51, 137
    pride, 9, 27, 28
    psychological effects of environment,
        8–10, 24
    security, 28, 74
    solitude, 28–30
    territorial imperative, 24, 93
    variety, environmental, 10, 36, 37, 39,
        46, 50, 137
    (*See also* Space)
Benches, 17, 21, 26, 27, 59, 60
Boat docks, 58
*Brief History of Parks and Recreation
    in the United States* (Doell and
    Fitzgerald), 4n.
Budget:
    construction, 60, 61
    maintenance, 61
    (*See also* Costs, minimizing)
Buildings, 14, 17, 46, 47, 63, 140

Campgrounds, 51, 58
Central Park, 2–4
Church, Thomas, 60
Circulation systems, 29, 30, 53, 59, 64,
    71–74, 136, 139
  artery types, 71, 136
  orientation points, 74
  parking lots, 14, 17, 20, 58, 135, 136
  roadway design, 20, 58, 62
  vehicular-pedestrian separation, 26, 136
Collaboration with landscape architects:
  behavioral scientists, 23-25, 28, 30
  building architects, 130
  facility operators, 59
  recreators, 1, 2, 6, 24, 60, 61
Colors (see Beauty)
Comfort, user, 59, 60, 76
Construction:
  budget, 60, 61
  costs, minimizing, 47, 61–63
  materials selection, 63–65, 139
  plans, 83, 84
Contours, 86–89
  (See also Slopes)
Costs, minimizing:
    construction, 47, 61–63
    maintenance, 18, 63–69

Demand studies:
  purpose, 22, 56
  questionnaire examples, 148–162
Design process, 79, 91–105, 107
  analysis: site, 99–102
    use-area relationships, 98, 99
  concept, 102–105
  inventory, 95–98
  program, 92–95
  refinement, 105
Design styles:
  contemporary, 6
  English Romantic period, 2, 3
  of Olmsted, 4, 5
Detail plans, 81, 83, 84
DeTurk, Phillip E., 129
Doell, Charles, 4n., 6, 7, 32
Drainage patterns, 31, 62, 95
Drinking fountains, 60, 77, 82
  (See also Furniture, park)
Dubos, René, 10

Elements of Park and Recreation
    Administration (Doell), 6n.

Elevation:
  drawings, 84
  as height expression, 88
Enclosure (see Space)
Experience:
  aesthetic (see Beauty)
  recreational, 5, 7, 8

Fees, landscape architectural, 109
Fitzgerald, Gerald B., 4n.
Forms (see Beauty)
Function, 31, 32, 42, 47–49
  creating efficiency, 54–78
  determining quality, 53, 54, 78, 79
Furniture, park, 18, 19, 60, 77, 82, 116
    benches, 17, 19, 21, 26, 27, 59, 60
    drinking fountains, 60, 77, 82
    light fixtures, 19, 82, 116
    sign styles, 21

Game area layout diagrams, 164, 165
Gradients:
  how indicated, 88, 99
  slope, 95
Grass, 58, 64, 65, 68, 141

Hall, Robert T., 26
Handball courts, 17, 164
Human needs (see Behavior, as influencing
    design)
Humidity, 58
  (See also Design process)

Intuition, designer's, 13, 35, 37, 92

Land:
  competition for, 10, 11, 16
  drainage, 62, 95
  shaping, 26, 47, 62, 63, 135 ·
  use, 16, 17, 47, 62
  (See also Contours; Design process)
Landscape architect:
  education, 5, 6, 91
  selecting, 108, 109
  title conception, 2
  (See also Collaboration with landscape
      architects)
Light fixtures, 19, 82, 116
  (See also Furniture, park)

Line weights, drawing, 85
Lines (*see* Beauty)

Maintenance, 59, 77
    costs, minimizing, 18, 63–69
Marinas, 14
Master plans, 81, 83, 84
Materials selection:
    construction, 63–65, 139
    plants, 14, 17, 62, 63, 65–68, 78, 165, 166
Models, scale, 84

Natural elements and forces, 14
    (*See also* Design process; Humidity;
        Plants; Rainfall; Snowfall; Soil;
        Sun; Water; Wind)
Nature study areas, 133, 141

Olmsted, Frederick Law, 2–5, 8
Open space, use of, 27, 70, 132
Order, environmental, 36–51, 137

Paine, Thomas, School-Park, 129
Park:
    definition of, 5, 6
    design goals, 7–10
    designer (*see* Landscape architect)
    planner (*see* Landscape architect)
    and recreation movement, 2–7
    system, 4, 78, 143–145
Park departments, 5, 6
Parking lots, 14, 17, 20, 58, 135, 136
Parkway, 5
*Personal Space: The Behavioral Basis of
    Design* (Sommer), 26
Perspective drawings, 84
Perverts, discouraging, 76, 78
Picnic areas, 16, 17, 58, 64
Plans:
    analyzing, 107–141
    case studies, 116–141
    construction, 83, 84
    creating (*see* Design process)
    detail, 81, 83, 84
    drawing, 85, 86
    master, 81, 83, 84
    planting, 83, 84
    preliminary, 105
    reading, 84–89, 137
    schematic, 82

Plans (*Cont.*):
    site, 82–84
    staging, 83
Planting plans, 83, 84
Plants, 14, 17, 62, 63, 65–68, 78, 165, 166
    (*See also* Design process)
Playgrounds, 17, 21, 22, 25, 64, 68, 75,
    132, 139–141
Preliminary plans, 105

Rainfall, 14, 58
    (*See also* Design process)
Recreation:
    definition of, 6
    departments, 5, 6
    movement (*see* Park and recreation
        movement)
    research, 23
Recreation areas, definition of, 5, 6
Ripley, Thomas H., 165
Riverside subdivision, 4
Roads (*see* Circulation systems)

Safety, 75, 76, 130, 131, 133
Scale:
    architect's, 88
    engineer's, 88
    human, 48, 49, 74
    speed, 49
Schematic plans, 82
School-parks, 55, 129–141
Section drawings, 84
Sign styles, 21
Silent Language, The (Hall), 26
Site, factors affecting design (*see* Design
        process; Land use)
Site plans, 82–84
Sizes, area, 54–56, 146–148, 163
Ski runs, 58
Slopes:
    as design factors, 16, 57, 58, 134
    how indicated, 88, 99
    maintenance of, 68
    orientation, 57, 58, 139
    (*See also* Contours; Design process;
        Land shaping)
Snowfall, 58
    (*See also* Design process)
So Human an Animal (Dubos), 10
Social gathering spaces, 26, 133
Social profiles, 29

Soil, 14, 17, 62, 63, 166–172
   (*See also* Design process)
Sommer, Robert, 26
Space:
   indoor, psychological effects, 40–42
   outdoor: functions, 42, 50
      psychological effects, 42–45, 62, 74
Staging plans, 83
Standards:
   activity, 21, 22, 146–148
   for area sizes, 54–56, 146–148, 163
   facility, 21, 22, 56, 57, 146–148
   park system, 143
Step design, 59
Sun, 14, 57
   (*See also* Design process)
Supervision, activity, 17, 69, 75, 139
Swamps, 16
Swimming areas, 17, 51, 76
Symbols, plan (*see* Plans, reading)

Tennis courts, 16, 17, 51, 56, 58, 62, 140,
   164
Territorial imperative, 24, 93
Territorial Imperative, The (Ardrey), 24
Textures (*see* Beauty)
Toboggan runs, 16, 139
Topography (*see* Contours; Design Process;
   Slopes)
Transition, environmental, 46, 47, 62

Use-area relationships, 14, 15, 17, 74–76,
   132, 135
   with site, 16–18, 47, 58, 62, 63, 134, 135
   with surroundings, 16, 18, 78, 134
   (*See also* Design process; Plans,
      analyzing)
User needs, determining, 22–24, 76
   demand studies, 22, 56, 148–162
   design program, 92–95
   (*See also* Behavior, as influencing
      design)

Vandalism, discouraging, 76–78
Variety, environmental, 10, 36, 37, 39, 46,
   50, 133, 134, 137
Vaux, Calvert, 4

Walkways (*see* Circulation systems)
Water, 14, 16, 17, 58
   (*See also* Design process)
Whistler, James McNeil, 38
Wind, 14, 57, 58, 133
   (*See also* Design process)
Working drawings (*see* Construction plans;
   Planting plans)

Yosemite Valley, 4